# On Pain and Suffering

# Lexington Studies in Classical and Modern Islamic Thought

**Series Editor: Hussam S. Timani**

This series explores and examines a vast literature on understudied strands in Islamic thought. The series topics include but are not limited to Qur'an and hadith studies, classical theological and philosophical doctrines, human knowledge, law and tradition, law and legal reforms, tradition and renewal, Salafi thought, piety movements, neotraditionalism, neoliberalism, neoreformism, neo-Islamism, cultural pluralism, and liberal and ethical humanism. Additional subjects for consideration are trends in contemporary Islamic thought such as democracy, justice, secularism, globalization, international relations, Islam and the West, and feminism. The volumes in the series examine, historicize, and analyze Muslim intellectual responses to the various trends of Islamic thought that have been under studied in Western scholarship. This series makes important and timely literature available to the English reader.

### *Titles in the Series*

*On Pain and Suffering: A Qur'anic Perspective*, by Abla Hasan
*Forging Ideal Muslim Subjects: Discursive Practices, Subject Formation & Muslim Ethics*, by Faraz Masood Sheikh
*Decoding the Egalitarianism of the Qur'an: Retrieving Lost Voices on Gender*, by Abla Hasan

# On Pain and Suffering

## A Qur'anic Perspective

Abla Hasan

Foreword by Jonathan E. Brockopp

LEXINGTON BOOKS
*Lanham • Boulder • New York • London*

Published by Lexington Books
An imprint of The Rowman & Littlefield Publishing Group, Inc.
4501 Forbes Boulevard, Suite 200, Lanham, Maryland 20706
www.rowman.com

86-90 Paul Street, London EC2A 4NE



British Library Cataloguing in Publication Information available

**Library of Congress Cataloging-in-Publication Data**

Names: Hasan, Abla, 1978- author.
Title: On pain and suffering: a Qur'anic perspective / Abla Hasan.
Description: Lanham: Lexington Books, 2021. | Series: Lexington studies in classical and modern Islamic thought | Includes bibliographical references and index.
Identifiers: LCCN 2021036048 (print) | LCCN 2021036049 (ebook) | ISBN 9781793650054 (cloth) | ISBN 9781793650061 (epub) | ISBN 9781793650078 (paperback)
Subjects: LCSH: Suffering—Religious aspects—Islam. | Pain—Religious aspects—Islam. | Qur'an—Criticism, interpretation, etc.
Classification: LCC BP190.5.S93 H37 2021 (print) | LCC BP190.5.S93 (ebook) | DDC 297.2/118—dc23
LC record available at https://lccn.loc.gov/2021036048
LC ebook record available at https://lccn.loc.gov/2021036049

™ The paper used in this publication meets the minimum requirements of American National Standard for Information Sciences—Permanence of Paper for Printed Library Materials, ANSI/NISO Z39.48-1992.

*To My Parents*

إلى الهرم
إلى ذكرى أبي رحمه الله
السيد إسماعيل عباس حسن
الشاكر أبدا
"و قليل من عبادي الشكور"
و إلى أخت الرجال
إلى أمي أطال الله عمرها
السيدة لمعان عبد الرحمن يوسف
الصابرة دوما
"و ما يلقاها إلا الذين صبروا و ما يلقاها إلا ذو حظ عظيم"
"رب ارحمهما كما ربياني صغيرا"

وَقَالَ الرَّسُولُ يَا رَبِّ إِنَّ قَوْمِي اتَّخَذُوا هَٰذَا الْقُرْآنَ مَهْجُورًا

*The Messenger has said, "Lord, my people treat this Qur'an as something to be shunned." (Q. 25:30)*

# Contents


Foreword xi

Acknowledgments xv

Introduction 1

Chapter 1: Rethinking the Beginning of the Journey: An Earthly Dwelling, Not Exile 5

Chapter 2: The Divine Assignment: The Divine on Earth 39

Chapter 3: Rethinking the Divine Status of Humans: A Key to Solving the Problem of Evil 61

Chapter 4: Rethinking the End of the Journey: Reevaluating Islamic Apocalyptic Literature 111

Conclusion 125

Bibliography 131

Index 137

About the Author 143

# Foreword

"The Qur'anic text confirms hardship as the core of the human earthly journey." With these words at the beginning of chapter 2, Abla Hasan lays the foundation for her analysis of the role of pain and suffering in religion. Put another way: Life is hard.

It may be little comfort to think that life is hard because God made it that way; couldn't God have made it easy instead? These and other similar questions are dealt with at length in this rich, complex book in which Professor Hasan walks the reader through some of the most vexing problems facing religious adherents today: what is the origin of evil? Why do we suffer? What awaits us at the end of time? And while this book is focused on the Qur'anic message, all will benefit from reading it. After all, pain and suffering are universal phenomena.

Even as I write this, thousands are still dying each day in a worldwide pandemic that has vexed us for more than a year, almost one billion human beings suffer extreme poverty and are chronically undernourished, and animal species are disappearing so fast due to pollution and climate change that scientists call this the sixth mass extinction. Even affluent societies suffer from epidemics of drug use, domestic violence, and suicide, and we all face death.

It would be reasonable to ask how the Qur'an, a book understood to have been revealed in Arabia over 1,400 years ago, could help us make sense of these issues. But in four beautifully organized chapters, Hasan finds Qur'anic insights on such subjects as the horrors of the Holocaust and the suffering of animals. While her conclusions will not be accepted by all, her arguments and careful explication of the text demand attention. Readers will come away with a new appreciation for the inimitable qualities of the Qur'an, the book that serves as her constant conversation partner.

In the footsteps of contemporary Qur'an interpreters Ziauddin Sardar, Nasr Hamid Abu Zayd, and Amina Wadud, Professor Hasan argues that the text must be wrestled with to render it relevant. Her first chapter is devoted to deconstructing common exegetical overlays, providing a clear canvas to begin her constructive work. In this chapter, she introduces her methodology of reading the Qur'an with "semantic minimalism," embracing its laconic style and rejecting expansions of the text common to traditional Qur'anic commentaries. Whatever we may think of the historical appropriateness or theological value of reading the Qur'an apart from traditional interpretation, it must be seen as an important exercise that helps to clarify the power of interpretive frames that have been traditionally placed on the text.

What Professor Hasan does not offer us is certainty. As she points out, "the human approach to religious reality is fallible, diverse, and relative." There is "no definite, apodictic, change-resistant epistemic religious knowledge that we can capture . . . at best, there are epistemic speculations." This brings us to the problem of religion itself which, she argues, is an "epistemic hardship." It is hard to overemphasize the importance of this insight. The very fact that we cannot know the reality of God, that we cannot know the Truth, drives us to keep delving into religious meaning. It also puts us into a position of epistemic humility. We may well believe that our religion is the right one, or that our interpretation of the Holy Book is the most accurate, but we cannot know this. For this reason, Hasan is quite clear in rejecting both a slavish acceptance of traditional Qur'anic interpretations and also a presumption of Islamic supremacy. Part of the epistemic hardship that is religion, she argues, demands that we each, independently, engage the religious text, that we do not blindly accept the authority of others.

This focus on individual responsibility also means that she rejects passive submission as the correct, pious response to worldly evil. In a remarkable chapter on eschatology, she criticizes popular Muslim narratives that describe a second coming of Jesus as a savior who will reject Christianity, accept Islam, and reign over a perfect, just order on earth. This is, she writes, "the use of hadith to invalidate the Qur'anic text." It also, in her view, unacceptably avoids human responsibility for facing and defeating evil as part of the divine test.

Nonetheless, precisely how human beings are to face evil remains unclear, and one hopes that Professor Hasan continues her analysis in a future volume. Particularly vexing is the problem of systemic evil, such as racism or climate disruption, where no specific evil actor is identifiable. It seems clear enough that religions enjoin one to take personal responsibility for their individual actions, but what do we do when the whole system is corrupt, where the mere act of driving to work or flying across the world to comfort one's dying parents accelerates climate change, for example?

These systemic issues are sometimes described as the result of inevitable human corruption, cited by Professor Hasan as one explanation for evil in the Qur'an. She writes, "in the Qur'an all unwanted outcomes can be categorized as the result of humanity's propensity for corruption, including that of the natural world, usually referred to as 'natural evil.'" In many societies, this notion of corruption even extends to the human body, where intersex bodies are regarded as 'defective' and surgically 'corrected' to conform with expected norms. Are these surgeons unable to recognize these bodies as divinely ordered? Or are they doing divine work by bringing corrupted bodies into order? Likewise, are farmers who burn down the Amazon forest corrupting the land? Or are they—are we all—doing divine work by extending agricultural land, superhighways, and subdivisions? In short, how can the Qur'an or any other holy text help us to recognize, and combat, forms of systemic corruption?

That such questions remain at the end of this book only underscores the fact that religion is an epistemic hardship. The paradox of the unknowable God means that theodicy is likewise unknowable, yet Professor Hasan does her best to make its outlines clearer. Part exegesis, part sermon, part rejection of past positions that have resulted in either quietism or discrimination, she assures us that "By going up against evil, which starts by understanding it first, we make our statement as God's gods on earth and reclaim our divinity." This, she says, is "the real meaning of our human journey."

Jonathan E. Brockopp
Pennsylvania State University

# Acknowledgments

I am heavily indebted to Dr. Jonathan E. Brockopp for his encouraging support and for his many valuable suggestions. I am grateful to Muhammad Ridwaan, director of Qalam editing, for his professional editing of this book and for his noble character. I am also thankful to Dr. Trevor Crowell, associate acquisitions editor for religion and Middle Eastern studies, at Lexington Books for the pleasure of finalizing this book with him. Deepest gratitude goes to Dr. Nora Peterson, chair of the Department of Modern Languages and Literature at University of Nebraska–Lincoln for her generous support of the writing of this book. Finally, finalizing this project was possible due to help and support from an anonymous reviewer who kindly provided me valuable feedback including a suggestion for the title.

# Introduction

While Islamic theology does not hold original sin to be a legacy inherited by humankind, paradoxically mainstream Islam still adopts almost all core elements of the Biblical account of the "fall of man." Adam, according to the traditional Islamic narrative, lived in paradise, but very soon sinned and disobeyed God as he and his wife, Eve, ate from a forbidden tree. As a punishment, they were expelled and sentenced—along with their offspring—to live on earth. According to this narrative, humanity began its worldly journey in exile. However, even a cursory glance at the traditional narrative can unearth underscrutinized blind spots and inconsistencies. While Islamic theology asserts that humans are not born sinners per se, they still have to bear the consequences of their father Adam's disobedience. Furthermore, the Qur'anic proclamation that Adam was forgiven and blessed for repenting to God does not necessarily equate with the rescindment of humankind's life sentence on earth.

Driven by a detailed hermeneutical investigation of the Qur'anic story of creation, I argue in this book for a questioning of the hybrid Biblical/Qur'anic narrative that gradually erased the lines that define the authentic Qur'anic account. Unfortunately, the popularity of the new hybrid story provides a problematic understanding of the story of creation. Despite the existence of terse exegetical voices that questioned the narrative, mainstream theologians allowed a monolithic account to pave the way for how the beginning of this human journey on earth is conceptualized. The story in its most traditional form, moreover, also dominates the manner in which the status of humans on earth is evaluated. As I conclude in this book, understanding pain and suffering for any possible existential reconciliation requires rethinking our adopted and our most trusted theological conceptualizations of the beginning of the journey, the end of the journey and even rethinking the main concept of Religion itself.

This book unveils internal textual inconsistencies and even contradictions in traditional interpretations and readings of the Qur'anic story of creation. As I conclude in this book, Adam was not created to dwell in paradise; rather, he was created from earth to live on earth. For the most part, two different stories in the Qur'an were misinterpreted as referring to two scenes in the same story; namely, the story of creation. While in fact—as this book proposes—there are two stories, the first is the story of Adam's creation, which takes place in paradise, and the story of Adam's disobedience, which takes place on earth. What is even more important than merely identifying the stories as two separate events is acknowledging the reason why the story of Adam's disobedience was narrated in Qur'an in the first place. His disobedience is not told for naught; rather, it unfolds in the same way all other prophetic stories are told in the Qur'an—for the many lessons and morals one can learn therefrom. Adam sinned but then repented to God, the way all of the penitent are encouraged to do. This is the didactic purpose of narrating the story of Adam, which is not shared to demonize or belittle Adam or his offspring, but to provide them—especially the sinners among them—with unfading hope and unwavering trust in God. Adam, as I argue in chapter 1, was never cursed by God, nor dismissed from paradise, the way the Devil was; rather, he started his divinely predestined journey on earth dignified as God's own "successor" (Q. 2:30). Adam and his offspring are God's most honored beings; as we read in the Qur'an, "We have honored the children of Adam" (17:70). We may have not started off our worldly journey on the wrong foot, after all!

This Qur'anic-based reinvestigation of the most momentous epoch in the history of humankind not only allows us a better understanding of the order of events but also provides a more robust approach to unlocking the real divine status of human beings as God's own deputies on earth. Humankind's earthly journey is not a form of exile but a divine mission. While epistemic intricacies essentially associated with the fulfillment of this divine mission are commonly cited as external undermining threats to the same idea of human religiosity, I argue in chapter 2 for an approach that implements these challenges instead. These challenges do not constitute a threat to the same concept of human religiosity but are best understood as an enthronement of it. Understanding the many hardships inextricably engraved in humanity's divine mission on earth provides a holistic approach in comprehending religion, both as humanly adopted and as historically processed.

Chapter 3 uses the argument for humanity's bona fide divine status, which I adopt in the first chapter and carry over into the second, as the bedrock from which to rethink one of the most nodal problems that any religious discussion can hardly escape, namely, the problem of evil. I divide this problem into "human evil" (otherwise known as "moral evil") and "divine evil" (or "natural evil"). I use the latter term to refer to evil caused by reasons that can't be explained by human evil. However, before embarking on such a thorny discussion, it is crucial to dismiss even in these early introductory remarks any intention of using my specific Qur'anic-based approach to theodicy to extrapolate ontological affirmations concerning the existence of God. Many have wrongly tried to use the existence of evil as an argument against the existence of God; therefore, it is important to clarify that in discussing the problem of evil I do not follow this tradition, but rather start from assuming the existence of God as an axiomatic ground for my argument. In other words, I don't aim to conclude by proving the existence of God, which, albeit an interesting argument, is beyond the scope of this work. Instead, I start by asserting His existence as a premise. Similarly, my argument against divine evil is not intended to qualify as an argument for the existence of God; rather, it aims at proving the existence of a *just* God. I am, therefore, more interested in discussing the conflict between the existence of an omnipotent God and the existence of evil. In short, while the question concerning evil is multifaceted, the question this book mainly explores is not one of ontology but of morality par excellence.

In chapter 4, I discuss the end of the human journey on earth as portrayed in mainstream Islamic apocalyptic literature. The detailed analysis provides a serious departure from the Qur'anic image, no less serious than the departure we find in the first chapter. In other words, revisiting humanity's real divine status in the Qur'an is used as an essential factor in reevaluating Islamic apocalyptic literature. As this book concludes, contrary to the Qur'an's basic crystallization of humanity's divine responsibility on earth as essentially personal, individual, and unavoidable, Islamic apocalyptic literature provides an approach to this responsibility that remains fictive, mimetic, and too problematic to be accepted as Qur'anic. While pain and suffering remain an unescapable individual and personal demarcation of our divinity, Islamic apocalyptic literature missed the point altogether when it advocated for collective escapes and eschatological happy endings.

In my investigation, I apply an internal analytic methodology of interpreting the Qur'an by using the Qur'an (*tafsīr al-Qur'ān bi-l-Qur'ān*). I start from and build on understanding the Qur'an—the way it is understood by the majority of Muslims—as "the speech of God, dictated without human editing."[1] This strict application is based on what I have previously referred to as "the semantic completeness of the Qur'anic language":

> By the "semantic completeness of the Qur'anic language" which I introduce as a strict application of using the Qur'an to interpret the Qur'an, I refer to the unmatchable sufficiency of the Qur'anic language, which makes all external

> semantic investigation of the meanings of words, terms, and expressions complementary in nature; these can come only second to the "best explanation" (Q. 25:33) that the Qur'anic text provides exclusively. According to the "semantic completeness of the Qur'anic language," the self-interpretive capacity of the Qur'anic text can be accessed as the most basic interpretive and epistemic tool to unlock the philological and the semantic nature of the Qur'anic text—a tool that derives its validity from God's commitment in the Qur'an itself to make reading and understanding the Qur'an accessible, as we read in: "We have made it easy to learn lessons from the Qur'an" (Q. 54:17) and in "it is up to Us to make it clear" (Q. 75:19).[2]

In order to clarify the real Qur'anic message, which is occasionally lost in interpretation, I adopt this strict research methodology, which dismisses any elements alien to the Qur'anic text.[3] I use one academic translation of the Qur'an, that of Muhammad A. S. Abdel Haleem (Oxford University Press, 2010). All other Arabic translations are by the author.

## NOTES

1. Malise Ruthven, *Islam: A Very Short Introduction* (Oxford: Oxford University Press, 1997), 21.
2. Abla Hasan, *Decoding the Egalitarianism of the Qur'an: Retrieving Lost Voices on Gender* (Lanham, MD: Lexington Books, 2019), 3.
3. Ibid. See introduction and chapter 1 in *Decoding the Egalitarianism of the Qur'an: Retrieving Lost Voices on Gender* for a detailed explanation and justification of the methodology I adopt in both books. This methodology constitutes one choice and does not indicate the exclusion of the validity of other research approaches that might use the Qur'an as *a recourse*, contrary to my treatment of the Qur'an as *the resource*.

# *Chapter 1*

# Rethinking the Beginning of the Journey

## *An Earthly Dwelling, Not Exile*

In this chapter I revisit the Qur'anic story of Adam and Eve. My circumspect hermeneutical investigation ends with exposing the fragility of the traditional exegetical understanding of the story. The traditional account, I argue, not only contradicts the Qur'anic text but devalues the real divine status that was originally assigned to humanity therein. My analysis reveals, a fortiori, inconsistencies and even contradictions in the story of Adam and Eve as commonly narrated. I end by proposing a new understanding of the account, one that is supported by the many Qur'anic evidence I put forward.

### THE TRADITIONAL ACCOUNT OF THE QUR'ANIC STORY OF ADAM AND EVE

According to the majority of Qur'anic interpretations, when Adam was created in paradise angels were ordered to prostrate before him. The Devil,[1] who was present, refused this divine order. "For this offense the devil is expelled from heaven."[2] Later, Adam and Eve, seduced by the Devil, disobeyed God, who afforded them countless blessings in heaven but prohibited them from approaching "one tree."[3] Therefore, as a punishment God sends both of them down from "the sky" to earth.[4] Adam—unlike the Devil, who was also sent to earth—repents and admits his mistake. The story ends by God granting Adam forgiveness and warning his offspring not to fall for the Devil's deceptions the way their father did.

The traditional account of the story clearly announces the beginning of human residency on earth as a punishment. In one way or another, earth is a place of exile to which Adam had to be sent for disobeying God. Furthermore, this exile doesn't end in Adam's lifetime, but is extended to his offspring, who will invariably have to deal with the consequences of their father's wrong choice. According to this story, human existence on earth can best be described as a mistake: Adam and his offspring were created to live in paradise; they were granted an unconditional right to happiness that Adam—and consequently his offspring—lost, when he disobeyed God. Clearly, this understanding of the story turns human existence on earth into a punishment, or worse still, a life sentence that humanity must endure in order to reclaim the right to what was first given to them unconditionally, namely, paradise. In other words, humanity's right to heaven or paradise turned—due to Adam's disobedience—from an unconditional gift to a reward that must be earned. The human journey on earth is marked by a divine judgment that determines who will be rewarded by making their way to paradise. Now, while some exegetical voices questioned the credibility of the story and wondered whether Adam's first garden was an earthly garden or was the same paradise he was created in, "the majority," as Ibn Kathīr (1300–1373) confirms, adopted the view that Adam's garden is the one in the heavens, which is the same eternal paradise.[5]

## PROBLEMATIC ASPECTS OF THE TRADITIONAL ACCOUNT

The traditional account of the story of Adam and Eve is problematic for many reasons. The story, as ascribed by Muḥammad Rashīd Riḍa (1865–1935) to his teacher Muḥammad ʿAbduh (1849–1905), caused a debate among Muslim scholars, as to whether *janna* refers to "a garden" or to "the promised paradise." Abū Manṣūr al-Māturīdī (853–944) affirms the difficulty of determining whether the garden Adam and Eve were asked to stay in is a worldly garden or the promised paradise, because "the verse doesn't include an explanation of that."[6] ʿAbduh doesn't hesitate in supporting the first opinion by saying, "Authenticating Sunni scholars adopt the first opinion."[7] Riḍā follows him in confirming that, while each party has its arguments, "what our teacher chose is the strongest opinion."[8] Ibn Qayyim al-Jawziyya (1292–1350) ascribes the same opinion to some scholastic theologians who held that the first dwelling Adam had was "not paradise but a garden that God prepared for him as a test."[9] Like ʿAbduh,[10] Ibn Qayyim ascribed this opinion to "Abū Ḥanīfa."[11] Al-Qummī ascribes to al-Ṣādiq the affirmation that Adam's garden was worldly.[12] While Muḥammad Mutwallī al-Shaʿrāwī (1911–1998) doesn't argue for an earthly garden per se, he refers to a garden that was prepared for Adam and Eve for a period of training before they finally started their earthly journey.[13] In that garden, Adam was taught "how to repent, how to ask for forgiveness and how to return to God."[14] More recently Muhammad Shahrour (1938–2019) argued for an earthly garden as well.[15]

In this section, I follow and expand this largely overlooked line of argument by questioning the logical consistency and preeminence of the mainstream interpretation of the story. While the full reconstruction of the more likely version of the story will follow this section, I begin by the assurance that Adam was not created to live in paradise, or what I refer to as the "heavenly garden"; rather, he was created to live on earth, or what I refer to as an "earthly garden." Adam was, as I prove in this chapter, created from earth to live on earth. This divine plan for Adam to occupy earth predated his disobedience. To be more specific, Adam was created to be sent down as a divine deputy to earth. The decision to send him to earth predated (and did not follow) his disobedience. However, before I can clarify what happened, I must explain the reasons I reject the traditional understanding of the story.

(1) The conspicuous announcement of the reason for creating Adam as *khalifa*, or successor, was made in Q. 2:30, as we read, "[Prophet], when your Lord told the angels, 'I am putting a successor (*khalīfa*) on earth.'" This Qur'anic description clearly asserts the divine intention of sending Adam as a successor to earth at the very same moment he was created. This happened before any sin or disobedience had taken place. The term *khalīfa*, or successive authority, is used in the Qur'an to affirm a meaning of authority that matches the previous meaning, "David, We have given you mastery (*khalīfa*) over the land. Judge fairly between people" (38:26).

Exegetical opinions—both traditional and modern—concerning the meaning of this divine intention and announcement to send Adam to earth as a *khalīfa* are divided into three. First, some interpreters proposed Adam as a successor to other beings like jinn that occupied the earth before him, which is the view Ibn Kathīr ascribes to ʿAbd Allāh ibn ʿUmar.[16] Fakhr al-Dīn Al-Rāzī (1150–1210) cites two possible meanings scholars offer for Adam being the "successor" in the previous verse: first, as a successor of jinn, who proceeded Adam in living on earth, and second, as a successor of God Himself.[17] While the first opinion lacks any textual support, both opinions buttress an earthly mission that was assigned to Adam the moment he was created and before any sin had taken place. Second, others interpreted the term as referring to successive authority among human beings themselves. For example, Ibn Kathīr, in *al-Bidāya wa-l-nihāya*, interpreted *khalīfa* by way of comparing it to Q. 10:14, "Later We made you their successors in the land, to see how you would behave."[18] This interpretation in itself affirms nothing but the fact that Adam and his offspring after him will be succeeding each other, generation after generation in existing on earth. Third, Adam was created as God's successor, or "deputy."[19] As Muhammad Husayn al-Ṭabāṭabāʾī (1904–1981) explains, the mentioned *khalīfa* is "the *khalīfa of God* Almighty."[20] Barbara Stowasser

(1935–2012) affirms the same opinion by saying, "the final version of the story in Sura 2, revealed in Medina, emphasizes that the purpose of Adam's creation was as God's 'vicegerent' on earth and tells of Adam's God-given higher knowledge."[21] Abu al-Qasim Mahmoud ibn Omar al-Zamakhsharī (1074–1143) refers to this meaning, too, as a probable explanation, "Adam was God's successor on his land."[22]

Now, the controversy of whether the intention behind the creation of Adam was to send him to earth as a successor to God Himself,[23] the view I support, or to succeed other beings that preoccupied earth before him, is not the key locus of this discussion. What matters most is the recognition that the announcement of the intention was mentioned the same moment Adam was created, or even shortly before that, and certainly before any sin had taken place. This means Adam's alleged heavenly sin, which took place after the divine avowal of the reason of his creation and after he allegedly lived in paradise for a while, was not the reason for sending him down to earth. Moreover, it was predetermined to be an earthly journey from the very beginning. Adam was created to be delegated to earth, not to dwell in paradise, as is commonly and incorrectly believed. Al-Shaʿrāwī supports this view by referring to the fact that "God specified Adam's mission before he was created."[24] Amina Wadud (b. 1952) rightly observes the same by saying, "It is clear from Qur'anic descriptions that the Garden was never intended as the dwelling place of the human species. Part of Allah's original plan in the creation of humankind was for man to function as a *khalifah* (trustee) on earth."[25]

(2) The clear and literal mention of "earth" in the process of creation indicates the journey as an earthly mission.[26] In other words, God created Adam not only knowing that He will send him to earth, but for the purpose of sending him to earth. This means that Adam's so-called heavenly disobedience was not the reason he was sent to earth; rather, Adam was created to be sent to earth. This perplexing mention of the word "earth" (*al-arḍ*) even before the act of disobedience takes place motivated Ibn ʿAbbās—who adopts the traditional interpretation of the story of Adam and Eve—to interpret the dialogue addressed by God to angels in Q. 15:28 and 2:30 as exclusively addressing a group of "ten thousand angels who were on earth at the time."[27] As he explains, Adam was created "to replace" them as his deputies on earth.[28] I reject this attempt to solve the problematic mention of "earth" even before the creation of Adam, for lacking any textual support.

The reevaluation of the order of events, as described in the Qur'an, can help us clear up the confusion. Three points must be considered here: First, the creation of earth predated the creation of heavens. Naming "earth" the moment Adam was created, in Q. 2:30, assures as Ibn Kathīr and the majority of exegetes confirm that "God started by creating the earth first and then created seven heavens."[29] This is also textually supported as we read in Q.

2:29, "It was He who created all that is on earth for you, then turned to the sky and made the seven heavens; it is He who has knowledge of all things." Second, in addition to the above textual confirmation, the creation of Adam as we can infer from the Qur'an took place after the creation of the heavens, as we read in one reference to both the earth and heavens in the story of creation. "Then He said, 'Adam, tell them the names of these.' When he told them their names, God said, 'Did I not tell you that I know what is hidden in the heavens and the earth?'" (2:33). The juxtaposition of both events assures that Adam's creation took place after and not before the creation of earth. Third, not only was the earth created before Adam, it was predesigned as a human dwelling. Let's read the following verse one more time, "It was He who created all that is on earth for you, then turned to the sky and made the seven heavens; it is He who has knowledge of all things" (2:29). The Qur'anic assertion that the earth was prepared and fully equipped with all that can make it a human dwelling is found in the expression "for you." This constitutes another assertion of a preexisting divine plan to send Adam to earth, one that preceded the act of disobedience.

(3) The heaven as described in the Qur'an is a permanent residence. It is a place where believers are promised eternity as we read in many places, including: "As for those who have been blessed, they will be in Paradise, there to remain as long as the heavens and earth endure" (11:108); and "The reward for such people is forgiveness from their Lord, and Gardens graced with flowing streams, where they will remain" (3:136). This view needs to be highlighted though for its contradiction with the traditional narrative of the story of Adam and Eve. First, the idea of this granted eternity seems to be ironic in light of the fact that Adam feared death—which was the very reason that motivated him to eat from the forbidden tree, as we read in Q. 20:120, "But Satan whispered to Adam, saying, 'Adam, shall I show you the tree of immortality and power that never decays?'" The concept of granted heavenly immortality contradicts Adam's interest in immortality in the first place. Why would he be interested in what he was already given? Why would he be terrified by an improbable idea? And why would the Devil use this claim as a strategy to seduce Adam? The fact that this is the reason Adam disobeyed God is an evidence that the place where he was at was not paradise, as incorrectly but commonly believed. Rather, Adam and his wife were already on earth, or an earthly garden.

ʿAbd al-Qādīr Shībah al-Ḥamd (b. 1921) defends the traditional account by arguing that paradise is awarded to the believers as a reward for their righteous deeds, but Adam was allowed to live in paradise before he did anything "as a test," which explains his exile.[30] I reject this attempt to justify Adam's exile because, while it solves the problem of the contradiction with paradise as an eternal residence, it creates another problem by suggesting paradise as a place to test Adam's faith. This, as I shall explain in detail, contradicts the Qur'anic confirmation of paradise as a place free from sin and legal obligations, and as a place of perpetual happiness as we read in Q. 42:22, "you will see them [evildoers] fearful because of what they have done: punishment is bound to fall on them—but those who believe and do good deeds will be in the lush meadows of the Gardens. They will have whatever they wish from their Lord: this is the great bounty." In an attempt to respond to a similar objection, Abu 'Abdullah al-Qurṭubī (1214–1273) argues that any sense of immortality in heaven is limited to believers who will be rewarded by entering paradise after the Day of Judgment. Otherwise, he argues, it might be an eternal place for some and a temporary place for others, according to whatever God decides.[31] I reject this opinion as well, because it is not supported by the Qur'anic text,[32] which to the contrary of his claim describes paradise differently. More recently, ʿAbd al-Ṣabūr Shāhīn (1929–2010) uses this difficulty to argue for an evolution of the human species and for prehuman ancestors who predated the creation of Adam and Eve. Both, he argues—contrary to the Qur'anic depiction of paradise—had "eternity as a dream" after witnessing the death and annihilation of their previous prehuman ancestors.[33]

In addition to the promised eternity in paradise, another question that deserves merit, here, is: What would be left of the concept of paradise, as a place of perpetual human happiness, if death and all its related fears and concerns are to be considered there? The logical contradiction between paradise as a place of eternal happiness and Adam's fear of death and his desire for eternity should motivate us to rethink the traditional account of the story of Adam. To come back to our point of departure, Adam must have been already on earth when seduced by Satan to eat from the forbidden tree. This is what explains his fear of death.

(4) In the Qur'an, there is no decisive linguistic term to refer to paradise that can allow us to end the controversy. This observation is very important, because many scenes that were interpreted as referring to paradise are those that happened on earth, in an earthly garden. Both paradise and Adam's first dwelling, which was an earthly garden, are referred to in the Qur'an as *janna*. In fact, the term *janna* can be used both in its wider Arabic acceptation and its Qur'anic sense to refer to paradise and to any garden. The term is only misinterpreted in some scenes as making an essential reference to paradise. If we check the way *janna* is used in the Qur'an we can easily infer that it can also refer to a "garden." Let us consider, for example, "If only, when you entered your garden, you had said, 'As God wills. There is no power not [given] by God'" (18:39). Therefore, the context of the verse is what should lead us to interpret it as referring either to the "heavenly garden" or instead the "earthly garden." To unravel the mystery, as I make clear in the next section, Adam was only created in paradise or in the heavenly garden. Subsequent events

take place on earth, in an earthly garden that God prepared for Adam as his first dwelling. In other words, Adam and Eve never dwelt in paradise—they were only created in paradise to be sent to earth. Paradise is the final abode that Adam and Eve and their righteous offspring will end up in after they successfully pass their earthly assigned test.[34]

(5) The Qur'anic story, unlike the traditional Biblical narrative of Adam and Eve, ends with God's forgiveness, which they were granted after their repentance, "Then Adam received some words from his Lord and He accepted his repentance: He is the Ever Relenting, the Most Merciful" (2:37). However, this forgiveness contradicts chastising them by way of sending them down to earth and depriving them from their otherwise unconditionally granted heavenly dwelling. How can God forgive Adam and still punish him with such a severe chastisement? What can be worse than sending someone to earth after they were granted a place in heaven? This particular difficulty challenges the traditional narrative by divesting forgiveness of its meaning. It is this difficulty that caused al-Qurṭubī to dismiss considering Adam's exile from paradise a punishment, "since he was expelled from paradise after He forgave him and accepted his repentance."[35] Instead, he refers to the eternal wisdom in testing Adam's offspring and stresses the meaning of "I am putting a successor on earth" (Q. 2:30) as a "noble virtue."[36]

(6) There is a deep theological contradiction between a punishment that includes Adam's offspring for what he did and the Islamic conceptualization of sin where "sin is viewed as individual and repentance is viewed as individual."[37] The traditional account of the story tampers with and even nullifies the repeated Qur'anic assurances of individual moral and ethical accountability that doesn't transfer to others. For example, in Q. 35:18 we read, "No burdened soul will bear the burden of another: even if a heavily laden soul should cry for help, none of its load would be carried, not even by a close relative." While Islamic theology accords great importance to individual responsibility, and does not follow Christian theology in adopting original sin as a well-established theological belief, this aspect of the traditional account of the story paradoxically echoes original sin in making all of humanity pay for a choice made by Adam and his wife. More importantly, the traditional account of the story cannot explain a deep logical contradiction between the Qur'anic portrayal of God as a just deity, "your Lord is never unjust to His creatures" (41:46), and the unfair punishment of Adam's offspring for what their father had allegedly committed.

(7) There is also a contradiction between the free access to paradise Adam was allegedly granted and the Qur'anic conceptualization of paradise as a merit-based human dwelling. The Qur'an literally asserts as much in many places, such as, "Hurry towards your Lord's forgiveness and a Garden as wide as the heavens and earth prepared for the righteous" (3:133). Therefore, the

concept of paradise as a free-access place, lost to Adam, must be reevaluated. According to the Qur'anic criterion, no one will enter heaven or hell unless led to either by their behavior. Heaven as a reward is a recurring theme throughout the Qur'an: "No soul knows what joy is kept hidden in store for them as a reward for what they have done" (32:17).

(8) There is a contradiction between paradise as an abode of ultimate happiness and the commandment of avoiding one tree as we find in the traditional account of the story. Duties, obligations, and commandments constitute hardship that a heavenly dwelling doesn't and shouldn't allow. Ibn Qayyim refers to this issue as the reason that motivated some scholars to argue for Adam's first dwelling as an earthly one, including Muḥammad ibn Bakr al-Iṣfahānī.[38] In addition, the command not to approach one tree contradicts a specific verse in the Qur'an, which promises believers that they will be granted anything they wish for in paradise: "you will see them [evildoers] fearful because of what they have done: punishment is bound to fall on them—but those who believe and do good deeds will be in the lush meadows of the Gardens. They will have whatever they wish from their Lord: this is the great bounty" (42:22). Clearly, Adam wished for eating from the forbidden tree. In a place where wishes are supposed to be granted, like the way the Qur'an describes paradise, Adam's wish should have been unconditionally granted, which is quite opposite to what we find in the traditional account of the story.

(9) There is a contradiction between paradise as a sin-free place, as it is described in the Qur'an, and the so-called sin committed by Adam there. In the Qur'an, believers are promised happiness in paradise that includes, among many other things, the absence of blame or reproach. In Q. 56:25 we read, "they will hear no idle or sinful talk (*ta'thīm*) there." The word *ta'thīm* comes from the root *a-th-m*, which means "to sin" through the act of blaming and reproaching. While believers are promised not to be reproached or blamed for anything in paradise, Adam was severely blamed, reproached, and even punished in the traditional account of the story.

Al-Qurṭubī responds to a similar objection, like the one I raise here, by saying, "their claim that paradise is a holy place, purified by God from sins, is a mere ignorance of their part. Because God ordered the Israelites to enter the holy land, Syria, which all people of all religions agree on its holiness. However, sins, apostasy, and lying have been seen in it and its holiness didn't prevent sins from taking place in it."[39] I reject this argument, which overlooks the fact that unlike the overt Qur'anic assurances of paradise as a sin-free place, the Qur'anic text never refers to any earthly holy place as free from sin. Describing some earthly places in the Qur'an as holy indicates other meanings, but the absence of sin is not one of them. However, those places are to be treated with special respect and according to special rules and rituals, which makes sinning a more plausible act in case those strict special rules are not strictly followed. For example, in the Qur'anic story of Moses he was ordered to take off his shows as he was entering the sacred valley of Ṭuwā as we read, "When he came to the fire, he was called: 'Moses! I am your Lord. Take off your shoes: you are in the sacred valley of Tuwa'" (20:11–12). In short, confusing what is holy and sacred to what is free from sin is a semantic twist foreign to the way the term is employed in the Qur'an.

(10) There is a contradiction between the traditional account of the story of creation—which assumes that Adam's sin is what caused him to be expelled from paradise—and the reference to the Day of Judgment in the Qur'anic scene, which describes the creation of Adam. According to this scene, the Devil, who refused the divine order to prostrate to Adam, challenged God that he will seduce Adam and his offspring and lead them to hell only if granted the chance to get his punishment postponed until the Day of Judgment. This problematic reference is made not once but in two places in the Qur'an:

> When We said to the angels, "Bow down before Adam," they all bowed down, but not Iblis. He retorted, "Why should I bow down to someone You have created out of clay?" and [then] said, "You see this being You have honored above me? If You reprieve me until the Day of Resurrection, I will lead all but a few of his descendants by the nose." (17:61–62)

And,

> We created man out of dried clay formed from dark mud—the jinn We created before, from the fire of scorching wind. Your Lord said to the angels, "I will create a mortal out of dried clay, formed from dark mud. When I have fashioned him and breathed My spirit into him, bow down before him," and the angels all did so. But not Iblis: he refused to bow down like the others. God said, "Iblis, why did you not bow down like the others?" and he answered, "I will not bow to a mortal You created from dried clay, formed from dark mud." "Get out of here!" said God. "You are an outcast, rejected until the Day of Judgment." Iblis said, "My Lord, give me respite until the Day when they are raised from the dead." (15:26–36)

The many references the previous verses make to the Day of Resurrection (Q. 17: 61), to the Day of Judgment (Q. 15:34), and to the day "when they are raised from the dead" (Q. 15:36) in a scene describing the creation of Adam that predates his sin and his so-called exile, should motivate us to rethink the story. In the scene of creation of Adam—before any sin had taken place—references collectively assure that a divine plan for Adam to be sent to earth to live, die and resurrected was already in place before he was even created. The Devil knew about the Day of Judgment and even death the moment Adam was created. This suggests the question: Was paradise really designed as an eternal dwelling for Adam? Or was he only created in paradise to be sent to earth according to a plan that included from day one references like death, returning to God, final resurrection, and final judgment?

All these contradictions between paradise as described in the Qur'an and the traditional account of the story of Adam and Eve should motivate us to open everything up to question and rethink the traditional interpretational approach to the story. As I mentioned before, the argument that the paradise from which Adam was exiled is different from the paradise prepared as the eternal dwelling for the righteous is not supported anywhere in the Qur'an. In addition, even if one accepts—for the sake of argument—that the paradise from which Adam was exiled was prepared as a dwelling for Adam, but then he lost his right to be there for sinning, the many differences between the way the Qur'an describes "paradise" and the paradise where Adam allegedly dwelled in the beginning leave us wondering about that place as "an indescribable great blessing" and as a place of ultimate happiness.[40] What is left to wish for, or even to miss, in a place where Adam receives orders to avoid what he longs for—where he has to grapple with evil and cunning temptation; where he fears death; where he is threatened by God Himself that he might lose his right to live in that garden any minute; where he makes mistakes and sins; where he is reproached by God; where he suffers shame and guilt; and finally, where he commits what he and his offspring will eternally regret! As I argue in the next section, Adam was created in paradise, yet he didn't dwell there, because it was not intended to be his initial residency. The story of Adam and Eve is best understood in two parts: first, the story of Adam's creation, which takes place in the heavenly *janna* or paradise; and second, the story of Adam's disobedience, which takes place in an earthly *janna* or garden. While I refer in this section to contradictions in the traditional understanding of the two stories, misunderstood as standing for two scenes in the same story, in the next section I refer to new evidence and observations that support the reconstructed story.

## RECONSTRUCTING THE STORY

In this section I argue for a new understanding of the Qur'anic story of Adam and Eve. Before we do so, it is important to clarify the traditional confusion that resulted in two stories—that is, the story of Adam's creation in paradise and the story of his earthly disobedience, to be treated as one story: first, misinterpreting the term *janna* as necessarily referring to paradise while—as I argued before—it can equally (and soundly) be used to refer to paradise or any garden, including earthly gardens like in Q. 18:33; second, the heavy dependence in exegesis on widely circulated Biblical narratives, or

Isrāʾīliyyāt (lit. "of the Israelites"), of the story of Adam and Eve. As Ramzī Naʿnāʿ explains,[41] this tendency to borrow from the Isrāʾīliyyāt includes rejected narratives that can neither be accepted by the appeal to human rational reason nor by the appeal to revealed scripture. Unfortunately, some Muslim exegetes borrowed almost all details from the Biblical story and kept adding them to the main body of the Qur'anic story until they ended up with a duplicated Biblical/Qur'anic account.[42] Jalāl al-Dīn al-Suyūṭī (1445–1505) provides an example of this uncited reference to the Biblical narrative:

> Satan approached Eve with a fruit and said: "Look at this tree. What a nice smell! What a delicious taste and what a beautiful color!" Then Eve took it and ate from it and went with the fruit to Adam to say: "Look at this tree. What a nice smell! What a delicious taste and what a beautiful color." Then Adam ate of it, and their private parts appeared to both of them. Adam hid inside a tree and was called by God who said: "Where are you?" Adam said: "Here I am." Then God said: "Come out." Adam said: "I am ashamed of myself." God said: "Get down to the earth" and then said, "O Eve, you seduced My servant. Therefore, you will suffer in pregnancy and in giving birth, and often will die doing this." Then God said to the serpent: "You are the one whom the Cursed [Devil] entered into to trick My servant. You will be cursed so your ends will be in your belly and you will never get any food other than dust. You and the offspring of Adam will be mutual enemies, wherever you find anyone of them you will chase [them] and wherever one of them finds you they will cut [off] your head."[43]

I refer to this exegetical deficiency as the "excessive exegetical narrativization of the Qur'an," which I have explained elsewhere as follows:

> This perplexing epistemic behavior of many exegetes was mostly based on the use of obsolete details (both authentic and inauthentic) from vaguely transmitted religious myths, preserved prophetic sayings, biblical narratives, and folk wisdom. Many times, this conglomeration of information was used to construct lengthier, more vibrant and entertaining Qur'anic commentaries. However, as expected, this behavior resulted in exegeses that were not fully reliable or authentic.[44]

Contrary to this tendency, in reading Qur'anic stories one should observe semantic minimalism as an essential stylistic character in the Qur'an. Many times, Qur'anic stories drop names of characters, heroes, places, and dates. Qur'anic stories are described in the Qur'an as "the best of stories" (12:3). However, this does not negate the independence of the Qur'anic story as a genre. What is mostly relevant here, out of all the distinctive features of Qur'anic stories, is their laconic approach to details. While storytellers invest their time crafting details that are commonly and positively viewed as the factor that brings stories alive and grabs audiences' interest, Qur'anic stories seem to be more selective, end-driven, and less concerned about such tactics. In our specific case, details both from Adam's creation and from his first dwelling in earth collectively, but wrongly, accumulated what is usually viewed as the continuity of the same plot. Qur'anic stories drop chronological order and many times allow events that can be tens or even hundreds of years apart to appear as if following each other. One thing is to be observed here: for sure, the Qur'an is not a book of history and should not be treated this way. Any approach to the unique style of the Qur'an that neglects this fact cannot extract the best results out of it. According to the Qur'anic criterion one basic question that each story tries to answer is the moral or the lesson one can learn from reading that story. Entertainment, amusement, and audience engagement are negatively viewed according to the Qur'anic criteria as distracting elements that can lead the audience astray. Qur'anic stories are shared for the lessons one can learn as we read, "There is a lesson in the stories of such people for those who understand" (12:111). And, "So [Muhammad], We tell you the stories of the prophets to make your heart firm and in these accounts truth has come to you, as well as lessons and reminders for the believers" (11:120). A basic question that any reading of the story of Adam and Eve should answer is: What is the moral of the story? Contrary to the traditional reading of the story that seems to be highlighting nothing but Adam's sin, the Qur'anic story itself clearly pinpoints the reason the story was shared in the first place. This happens in Q. 7:27 as the verse wraps up the story with a warning addressed to Adam's offspring not to be deceived by Satan the way their parents were deceived and misled by him. Third, is the excessive use of hadith. In the hadith collection of Muḥammad ibn Ismā'īl al-Bukhārī (810–870), one *ṣaḥīḥ* (sound) hadith portrays Moses addressing Adam as "our father who failed us and caused us to be expelled from paradise because of your sin."[45] The excessive usage of the prophetic tradition, which started by the desire to explain the Qur'anic text and ended by the unauthorized deactivation of some of what was confirmed in the Qur'an, found its way to the story of creation the way it found its way to many core theological beliefs and practices. This is another exegetical shortcoming that I refer to as "the use of hadith to invalidate the Qur'anic text."

> Hadith was supposed to play only a minor role in terms of explaining the Qur'an. The Qur'an itself indicates this by describing the Qur'anic text as "clear" (Q. 2:99), consistent, "if it had been from anyone other than God, they would have found much inconsistency in it" (Q. 3:82), and as fully explained, "we have explained it on the basis of true knowledge" (Q. 7.52). Unfortunately, the unjust categorization of the Qur'anic text as profoundly abstruse text,

> allowed scholars to use hadith as a necessary tool to unlock its ambiguities, until it gained a prioritized status almost equal to the Qur'anic text itself.[46]

Fourth, the "fallacy of exegetical semantic satiation." The Qur'anic narrative style only superficially might seem as if repeating the same scenes, passages, and whole stories. A general but frequently occurring misunderstanding of the Qur'anic style is epitomized in the following statement, "The most significant aspect to emerge in the literature related to the stories of the prophets is, undoubtedly, the definition of a linear chronology. The Qur'ān presents passages in open order, with frequent repetitions of the same episode in more than one *sūra*."[47] The Qur'an is best to be treated as an independent genre that doesn't follow ordinary rules of narration. Keeping in mind this unique scriptural characteristic can help avoid much of the frustration in reading the Qur'an, which Jane McAuliffe (b. 1944) explains by saying,

> Expectations of how a "scripture" or a "classic" should be structured—how it should "read"—contribute to the frequently experienced frustration. European and North American readers almost inevitably bring to the reading of the Qur'an biblically formed assumptions that "scripture" will behave in a certain way, will have a narrative structure, will move forward in time, will assemble its genres into distinct sections.[48]

Qur'anic stories don't follow one basic structure; rather, they usually consist of scattered scenes that follow but never repeat each other. Therefore, reading Qur'anic stories requires an active effort of gathering and organizing to end up with a narrative that can be told from the beginning to the end.

> Many times [. . .] repeated words, phrases and scenes, or what might sound like repeated scenes in the Qur'an are commonly treated as indicating the same exact meaning. However, in a book like the Qur'an, believed by Muslims to be a literal miracle, rethinking repetition can unearth many hidden messages that have been gone inaccurately interpreted for so long.[49]

Repetition in the Qur'an remains as a valid subject of inquiry; interpreting different verses from the story of Adam and Eve as simply repeating the same scene is one reason that can explain the exegetical confusion in terms of interpreting the story.

Fifth, an exegetical deficiency I refer to as "the authoritative approach to the Qur'an." As Ibn ʿĀshūr (1879–1973) makes clear in his *tafsīr*, the majority of scholars argue that Adam's garden is the same "eternal paradise" God promised the righteous believers.[50] Like many other Sunni exegetes, Ibn Taymiyya (1263–1328) disparages thinking of Adam's first dwelling as an earthly one. He belittled this view by ascribing it to philosophizers, atheists, innovative scholastic theologians, and Muʿtazilites! He summarizes his rejection as the following, "Both the book [the Qur'an] and the Sunna refute this opinion. In addition, the ancestors of this *umma* along with their Imams agree on its falsehood."[51] However, while thinking of the eternal paradise as Adam's first dwelling was historically considered a foregrounded view, very little is known about a glossed-over view that audaciously contended the soundness of that opinion. Because while mainstream consensus agreed on a heavenly image of the garden Adam was first placed in, an interesting view that al-Ṭabāṭabāʾī vaguely ascribes to some of "Āl al-Bayt [People of the Prophetic House]" suggests earth and not paradise as Adam's first residence.[52] In one way or another, Qur'anic exegeses have been harvesting the results of the hegemony of Sunni Ashʿarī theology and the claim to an exclusive right to sound *tafsīr.* This suspicious and even entrenched attitude at times might partially explain the relegation of many valuable interpretive contributions as they were simply labeled as unorthodox. Unfortunately, like in our specific case many times, "debates among scholars themselves concerning whose interpretation should be given precedence were sometimes resolved by a partial or even a complete marginalization of many linguistic based exegeses, and were never fully recovered."[53]

At this point I start referring to not one but two stories. The first story describes the creation of Adam in paradise. I refer to this as "the story of creation." Roughly speaking, all events of this story take place in paradise or in the heavenly garden. This story starts by the divine announcement of creating Adam as God's own deputy on earth and ends by the Devil's sole dismissal from paradise. I distinguish this story from the story of Adam's disobedience, which takes place in his first earthly dwelling on earth in an earthly garden. I call this story "the first test." At this early stage, one can easily conclude that the term "the fall of Adam" doesn't have any equivalent in my proposed dichotomy. In addition to the ten previously mentioned contradictions that motivate one to rethink the reliability of the traditional narrative, a further ten constructive reasons as to why a reconsideration of the story should be considered are discussed at length in the following.

(1) The angels' reaction to the divine announcement: the special assignment of Adam[54] as the divine successor on earth seems to have alarmed angels who had reasons to mention in an attempt they made –probably—to motivate God to think of them as a more suitable candidate for such an honor. The angels' response to God's announcement of His intention to send Adam as a divine successor took the form of a comparison they made between Adam and themselves. As we read in the Qur'an, they said, "How can You put someone there who will cause damage and bloodshed, when we celebrate Your praise and proclaim Your holiness?'" (2:30). In fact, this part of the dialogue confused and puzzled many interpreters. How did angels know the moment Adam was

created that he will be responsible for bringing about earthly damage and bloodshed? Was this statement solely based on their intuition or did they have an empirical experience of Adam's bloody nature? Are angels provided foreknowledge? Furthermore, what motivated the angels to say what they said to God as He announced His reason for creating Adam? Al-Zamakhsharī refers to commonly proposed answers that we find across different books of *tafsīr*: First, he refers to the possibility that angels protested against choosing Adam because they had already been informed by God about Adam's bloody nature. Second, some proposed that angels knew about what will happen due to their access to the "Preserved Tablet." Third, they protested due to their knowledge that all other beings—other than they—would be fallible and different from the pure nature they are solely provided with. Fourth, they compared Adam and his offspring to the jinn, who predated Adam in living on earth.[55] Ibn ʿĀshūr rejects those interpretations in his explanation of the verse and refers instead to the angels' pure intuition that enabled them to make such a prediction because "their perceptions are ultimately supreme due to their being devoid of material impurities."[56]

While some of the previously mentioned proposals sound more convincing than others, I argue that almost all of them should be rejected for lacking Qur'anic textual justification. In addition, to the contrary of what we read in some proposed answers many clear Qur'anic indications assert the opposite. Angels, as we learn from the Qur'an, don't have foreknowledge and are not provided special intuitive abilities, for they themselves admitted that: "They said, 'May You be glorified! We have knowledge only of what You have taught us'" (2:32). Abu Zayd'Abd al-Raḥmān al-Thaʿālibī (1384–1479) denies angels having access to foreknowledge and asserts the following statement as equally applicable to all angels, "we have learned for sure that angels don't know the unseen."[57] Foreknowledge, as the Qur'an confirms, is a divine quality that no one but God can have access to: "He has the keys to the unseen: no one knows them but Him" (6:59). In addition, the reference to the jinn or any other beings that predated Adam's occupation of earth should be rejected for two reasons: first, because it is not textually supported and second, because of the problematic judgment and unjust bias involved in the comparison the angels allegedly made between beings they already know and the newly created being, Adam.

While not all aspects of the unseen can be equally determined, including the exact intention of the angels as they responded that way to God's announcement, what is clear from the Qur'an though is the high rank that was assigned to Adam, which qualified him to be chosen as God's successor on earth. This was made clear once angels were ordered to prostrate to Adam. ʿAbduh—as Riḍā narrates—clarifies the confusion caused by interpreting the order as an order to "worship Adam"[58] and explains "that prostration was not a prostration of worship, because no one can be worshipped except for God."[59] While I agree that the order is not to be understood as an order to worship Adam, I reject also his understanding of the order as an order to "submit to" Adam.[60] The order to prostrate was an order to submit to God by confirming God's divine choice and is better understood as a gesture of approving Adam's divine status, which the angels—unlike the Devil—ended up doing. In fact, as we read in the Qur'an, the prostration was conditioned by God's assignment of Adam as divine, which was done by way of breathing His spirit into him, "When I have fashioned him and breathed My spirit into him, bow down[61] before him" (15:29). This clarifies that the order was not to glorify Adam himself as much as it was to glorify the "divine Adam"; or, in other words, it was to glorify the "divine in Adam." The angels, by responding to the order, expressed their submission to God by submitting to the divine choice to choose Adam as a divine deputy. The Devil, on the other hand, refused God's choice by rejecting the order to prostrate. It was divinely offensive because "The offense of non-prostration is not an offence against the object of prostration, the human, but against the creator of that human, against God. The importance of the human is invested in the fact that God made it. Further, God made it with God's own hands."[62]

However, this approval and submission happened only after the angels initiated what sounds like an attempt to negotiate finalizing Adam's divine assignment as God's successor. They said, "'How can You put someone there who will cause damage and bloodshed, when we celebrate Your praise and proclaim Your holiness?'" (Q. 2:30). The angels were probably comparing themselves to Adam in an implicit attempt to suggest themselves as a better fit for that honorable assignment. Therefore, when they mentioned bloodshed and damage, they only compared what they do, which is praising God and proclaiming His holiness, to what they are incapable of doing, which is bloodshed and damage. The angels in this verse did not, and could not, in fact reveal anything about Adam. Rather, they were merely reflecting on their own nature and describing themselves. They simply described what they can and cannot do. The angels in this verse are not concerned with objecting to choosing Adam as much as they are interested in proposing themselves as the most fitting choice. What supports this argument for an implicit desire that the angels had to be assigned as the divine deputy on earth instead of Adam is a specific expression in the conversation between God and the angels, "'Did I not tell you that I know what is hidden in heavens and the earth, and that I know what you reveal and what you conceal?'" (Q. 2: 33). While the verse "doesn't explain what the angels concealed,"[63] the subtle reference to something the angels concealed confirms a desire to be chosen instead of Adam, whom they thought themselves "to be better than him."[64] However, due to their pure angelic nature this desire didn't motivate them to disobey God the way the Devil did.

(2) The meaning of "names" in Q. 2:31–33: Another puzzling peace in the scene of creation is the meaning of "names":

> He taught Adam all the names [of things], then He showed them to the angels and said, "Tell me the names of these if you truly [think you can]." They said, "May You be glorified! We have knowledge only of what You have taught us. You are the All Knowing and All Wise." Then He said, "Adam, tell them the names of these." When he told them their names, God said, "Did I not tell you that I know what is hidden in heavens and the earth, and that I know what you reveal and what you conceal?" (2:31–33)

What does "names" here refer to? And why did God challenge the angels by Adam's ability to name what they could not? What does the ability of naming really stand for? Interpretations of the meaning of "names" varied among exegetes. According to many, including Ibn Kathīr, God taught Adam "names of all things: names of things themselves and names of their related acts."[65] ʿAlī b. Muḥammad al-Māwardī (972–1058) summarizes exegetes' opinions regarding the meaning of teaching Adam all "names" as including teaching Adam: names of angels, names of Adam's offspring, and names of all things.[66] The third opinion, as he explains, includes the following options: First, God taught Adam names without teaching him their meanings. Second, God taught Adam names along with their meanings and references, because learning names without their meanings is useless. ʿAbduh, followed by Riḍā, interpreted teaching "names" as referring to teaching their "references."[67] Al-Shaʿrāwī asserts the process as referring to the possibility that Adam was taught all names after their references were created by God. He applies this to the ability of naming new things, which Adam's offspring derive from their already taught names. For him, all new names that enter any language don't develop in a vacuum; rather, they develop within each language.[68] Muhammad al-Shanqīṭī (b. 1966) asserts this as the right meaning as well.[69] A more general interpretation of the meaning of names, as referring to humans' superior knowledge and as asserting their divine nature, was mentioned by Stowasser:

> Thus, while created from matter, Adam's nature included a divine breath, a spark, which God granted to the human beyond all other creatures. This higher nature conferred dignity and also obligation. The Qur'an states this by saying that God's purpose in Adam's creation was to make him God's vicegerent (*khalifa*) on earth (2:30). He endowed Adam with creative knowledge about the natures of things by teaching him "the names, all of them" (2:31), so that Adam's knowledge was above that of the angels (2:32–3);

and God commanded the angels to prostate themselves before Adam. Only Iblis refused to acknowledge the human's superiority and instead asserted his own.[70]

Al-Rāzī, however, mentions what he calls "the most famous opinion"[71] on the meaning of "names" in Q. 2:31. As he asserts, the term refers to "all different languages used by Adam's offspring today."[72] According to this view, the children of Adam used all these languages, but when he died and as they spread, each of them started to use only one language until they forgot each other's languages. To conclude, "God is He who taught Adam names"[73] is a theme that we find to be repeatedly referred to. In addition, interpreting "names" as "languages" is also a recurring theme that we have seen. However, there is a hitherto uncited part in the verse that requires explanation. Adam's ability of naming things as we read in Q. 2:31–33 was uniquely bestowed to him. Or, as we read in the Qur'anic text, it was more of a challenge to the angels. Two things are to be stressed here: first, the Qur'an asserts language as an *innate* ability and second, it asserts language as an innate *human* ability. The angels were not able to understand Adam's language. They confessed that to God by admitting that they can know only what they are taught by God. Interestingly enough, both attributes find a perfect match in Noam Chomsky's (b. 1928) well-known theory of universal grammar. According to Chomsky, "the ability to acquire and use language is a specific human capacity."[74] But Adam was not taught by God only one language. He was taught all "names," which I follow many exegetes in interpreting as referring to "human earthly languages." Adam and all humans, then, are provided an innate ability to speak any human language. According to Chomsky's theory, "universal grammar" is defined as, "the study of the conditions that must be met by the grammars of all human languages."[75] Every human being is born already provided knowledge of universal grammar, or, put differently, universal grammar is hardwired into human brains. In fact, rethinking this part of the scene adds to the reasons I have for arguing for earth and not paradise as the initial dwelling God prepared for Adam before he sinned and even before he was created. In this section, I argue for "names" as referring to the innate ability of speaking all "human languages" used on earth; the ability that Adam was divinely provided with. I use another two verses from the Qur'an to dismiss "references" as a plausible interpretation of "names" in Q. 2:31. In Q. 53:23, the Qur'an's polemic against pre-Islamic polytheism names some goddesses only to describe them as mere "names" by using the same term as we find in Q. 2:31. "[Disbelievers], consider al-Lat and al-'Uzza, and the third, other one, Mannat—are you to have the male and He the female? That would be a most unjust distribution!—these are nothing but names [*asmā'*] you have invented yourselves, you and your forefathers" (53:19–23). Referring to goddesses as names with no references or as made-up names should motivate us to reconsider the necessary nexus some interpreters suggested between teaching Adam names of things and their references. The names of the three goddesses in the Qur'anic usage here is better understood as what is referred to as "empty names" or "non-referring names."[76] Second, as we read in Q. 7:70–71 in the midst of a dialogue between Noah and his people, we find the same meaning ascribed to names (*asmā'*), "They said, 'Have you really come to tell us to serve God alone and to forsake what our forefathers served? If what you say is true, bring us the punishment you threaten.' [71] He said, 'You are already set to receive your Lord's loathing and anger. Are you arguing with me about mere names [*asmā'*] [of idols] you and your forefathers invented, names [*asmā'*] for which God has given no sanction? Just wait; I too am waiting.'" The objection that the Qur'an may be referring to the three concrete idols which pre-Islamic Arabs used to visit and worship doesn't correspond to the fact that what the Qur'an was attacking was the divinity of those idols, which allowed for such practices in the first place. In other words, the three names are empty in terms of their ability to refer to real deities—which is what the Qur'an was mostly interested in attacking—not in terms of their semantic functionality as proper names referring to three polytheistic objects or shrines. "Names" in Qur'anic usage is a linguistic term that does not essentially involve or require references. In the story of creation itself, names stand for languages. Adam was taught human languages to use in his earthly journey, or, in other words, Adam was provided with an innate ability to speak human earthly languages. The uniqueness of these languages as exclusively human is what made it a challenging task for the angels to understand them.

(3) The meticulousness of the Qur'anic switch in naming the Devil from Iblīs to Shayṭān: The Qur'an makes a distinction between the Devil—often loosely referred to as Satan—as Iblīs and then as Shayṭān. This distinction, as I prove here, adds to the many reasons we should consider rethinking the story of Adam and Eve. More importantly, this distinction provides for us guidance on how to sort out heavenly scenes that took place in paradise and earthly scenes that took place in Adam's first dwelling. The way the Devil is named in the Qur'an draws the line that needs to be recognized between the story of creation and the first test. What is the difference between Iblīs and Shayṭān? What explains the Qur'an's switching between the two names? Unfortunately—unlike the Qur'an—many *tafsīr* books and scholars seem to use the two terms interchangeably, to wrongly suggest that Satan "is sometimes used as another name or attribute of Iblis."[77] For example, Ibn ʿĀshūr refers to the Devil as Shayṭān to describe how he "felt frustrated when asked to prostrate to Adam."[78] Similarly, we find in the *tafsīr* of Ibn ʿAbbās an accusation that ascribes temptation to the Devil when named Iblīs.[79] While there are many others available, I confine myself to these two examples, which—as

I prove in this section—have wrongly named the Devil the opposite way in both cases.

In his discussion of the difference between Iblīs and Shayṭān, Whitney S. Bodman refers to a suggested distinction made between an actor and a character. According to this distinction, Shayṭān "is an actor, a participant in a story, who plays a role but never develops. He is a consistent representative of the force of evil."[80] On the other hand, Iblīs "is commonly a character, the focal point of a story, who develops a personality that evolves and responds to shifting situations."[81] As he explains, Iblīs shows elements of development as a character in the Qur'an. Bodman also refers to another way of describing the difference between the two terms in that they signify two distinct discourses about the nature of evil.

> In the case of al-Shayṭān, he is the permanent opponent of humankind. His personification of evil is generally without qualification or countervailing virtue. He is wholly evil, wholly dark, and wholly cursed. He has always been evil. He always will be.
>
> This is not the case with Iblīs, who conveys a more human demeanor. [. . .] Further, since Iblīs is by many accounts a *jinn*, who by nature can be either good or evil, Iblīs has a certain degree of comparability with the human condition. He went astray as humans change.[82]

In his analysis of Iblīs as a character he refers to him not as evil per se but as "a tragic character."[83] Therefore, like other tragic characters, "it is the audience—in this case the reader—who decides what is tragic. The character of Iblīs and the meaning of his story will be determined by the reader's response to it, which is why a consideration of the nature of narrative and the enterprise of reading becomes so critical to an understanding of Iblīs."[84]

Torsten Löfstedt makes another attempt to draw a distinction between the two terms, as he says,

> I suggest that the relation between the terms "Iblis" and "Shaytan" is the same as that between the Devil and "demon." "Shaytan" occasionally occurs as a count noun rather than a proper name in the Qur' an; the plural form is found (Q6.112); as is the indefinite form in Q81.25 "an accursed devil" and Q15.17 "every cursed devil." According to Muslim belief, every individual has a shaytan who tempts him; Kister quotes a tradition according to which Muhammad said: "My satan was an unbeliever but God helped me against him and he converted to Islam; my wives were a help for me. Adam's satan was an infidel and Adam's wife was an aid in his sin" [53]. Ultimately it is Iblis, who is responsible for all temptations, as these narratives specify, but the individual experiences these temptations as coming from one of his minions.[85]

The hermeneutical investigation of the way the Qur'an refers to the Devil as Iblīs and Shayṭān reveals three things: First, the two terms are not synonyms and therefore they shouldn't be used interchangeably. A strict Qur'anic reading of the story should not overlook the distinction the Qur'an itself makes between the two terms. Second, the Qur'anic distinction between the two terms supports the argument for a distinction that should be made between the story of creation, which takes place in paradise, and the story of the first test, which talks place on earth. Third, the Qur'anic exclusive usage of the two terms supports the existence of a change that occurred to the Devil, which allows for switching from his designation as Iblīs to his designation as Shayṭān. This change is not a change in the Devil's character though—which appears to be systematically viewed in the Qur'an—or a change from a proper name to count number[86] but a spatiotemporal change and a major substantial transformation that has to do with the Devil's earthly journey. As I prove in the following, the Devil is referred to in the Qur'an as Shayṭān in all scenes associated with his existence on earth and referred to as Iblīs in all heavenly senses. In fact, this terminological distinction is crucial in helping us sort out which Qur'anic scenes belong to the story of creation and which scenes belong to the first test.

Let's consider the following essential observations on the way the two terms are used in the Qur'an. First, in the Qur'an we find the term Iblīs to be used in scenes related to Adam's creation in paradise. Many Qur'anic references support using the term Iblīs to designate the Devil in his pre-earthly existence. We find as much in the following verses: "When We told the angels 'Bow down before Adam,' they all bowed. But not Iblis, who refused and was arrogant: he was disobedient" (2:34); "We created you, We gave you shape, and then We said to the angels, 'Bow down before Adam,' and they did. But not Iblis: he was not one of those who bowed down" (7:11); "We created man out of dried clay formed from dark mud—the jinn We created before, from the fire of scorching wind. Your Lord said to the angels, 'I will create a mortal out of dried clay, formed from dark mud. When I have fashioned him and breathed My spirit into him, bow down before him,' and the angels all did so. But not Iblis: he refused to bow down like the others. God said, 'Iblis, why did you not bow down like the others?'" (15:26–32); "When We said to the angels, 'Bow down before Adam,' they all bowed down, but not Iblis. He retorted, 'Why should I bow down to someone You have created out of clay?' (17:61); "We said to the angels, 'Bow down before Adam,' and they all bowed down, but not Iblis: he was one of the jinn and he disobeyed his Lord's command" (18:50); "When We said to the angels, 'Bow down before Adam,' they did. But Iblis refused" (20:116); "Your Lord said to the angels, 'I will create a man from clay. When I have shaped him and breathed from My Spirit into him, bow down before him.' The angels all bowed down together, but not

Iblis, who was too proud. He became a rebel. God said, 'Iblis, what prevents you from bowing down to the man I have made with My own hands? Are you too high and mighty? Iblis said, 'I am better [than] him: You made me from fire, and him from clay.' 'Get out of here! You are rejected: My rejection will follow you till the Day of Judgement!' but Iblis said, 'My Lord, grant me respite until the Day when they are raised from the dead'" (38:71–79).

Second, in Q. 26:94–95 we find the term Iblīs used to describe the gathering of those demons who followed and supported Iblīs on the Day of Resurrection after the annihilation of the earthly physical world: "and then they will all be hurled into Hell, together with those that misled them, and all Iblis's supporters." The term Iblīs is precisely used here to make an unmistakable connection between those whom the Qur'an identifies as the supporters of Iblīs and his pre-earthly challenge to God that he made in paradise, when he was Iblīs. Here, the Qur'an makes a distinction between being a follower of Iblīs and a follower of Shayṭān. Followers of Iblīs are more connected to the fulfillment of his initial challenge to God. This is to be distinguished from the mere human following of Shayṭān; a more common and a more often recurring theme and warning we find in many places in the Qur'an.

Third, Q. 34:20 asserts the argument for the name Iblīs as used to designate the Devil in his pre-earthly, extraterrestrial existence by using the term Iblīs in a retrospective reference made to the Devil's heavenly challenge to God (Q. 7:16). In Q. 34:20, we read, "Satan [Iblīs][87] was proved right in his opinion of them, for they all followed him—except for a group of believers—even though he had no authority over them." Now, let us consider what we read in Q. 7:16, "And then Iblis said, 'Because you have put me in the wrong, I will lie in wait for them all on Your straight path: I will come at them—from their front and their back, from their right and their left—and You will find most of them are ungrateful.'" By comparing the two verses it is clear that Q. 7:16 makes a reference to what the Devil thought and to his opinion when he was Iblīs, I mean when he was still in paradise and before he started his earthly journey as Shayṭān. Therefore, the verse precisely uses the term Iblīs.

Fourth, and interestingly enough, in the rest of the Qur'an we find the term Shayṭān and not Iblīs used to designate the Devil in his earthly journey. It is Shayṭān and not Iblīs whom the Qur'an names in the many references to the worldly battle the Devil launches against Adam and his offspring. The term, unlike Iblīs, comes both in the singular form and in the plural and applies both to the jinn and humans. This is the reason that motivated some to wrongly interpret the term Iblīs as referring to the head or chief of all devils.

Fifth, the most important observation out of all of the above is a precise, immediate shift that the Qur'anic text makes in the same scene from using Iblīs to Shayṭān in a clear and unmistakable reference to the end of the heavenly scene and the initiation of the earthly scene. This textual reference is a clear demarcation of where the story of the creation ends to allow the story of the first test to begin. Let's consider the overlooked linguistic shift in the following verses, "When We said to the angels, 'Bow down before Adam,' they did. But Iblis [Iblīs] refused, so We said, 'Adam, this is your enemy, yours and your wife's: do not let him drive you out of the garden and make you miserable. In the garden you will never go hungry, feel naked, be thirsty, or suffer the heat of the sun,' But Satan [Shayṭān] whispered to Adam, saying, 'Adam, shall I show you the tree of immortality and power that never decays?' and they both ate from it" (20:116–20). The paradoxical shift in the previous dialogue from referring to the Devil as Iblīs to Shayṭān is not pointless or random.[88] In fact, as mentioned before, it provides us with a clear indication on how and when to draw a line between what happened in paradise and what happened on earth. It is also relevant to mention that Q. 7:20–22 uses Shayṭān and not Iblīs to refer to events that took place on earth and not paradise as it is commonly but wrongly believed.

(4) The Devil's individual exile from paradise: This observation builds on the previously mentioned linguistic distinction that should be made between Iblīs *and* Shayṭān. However, this observation is more logical in its nature and less linguistic in its core as a concern. The order given to Iblīs to leave paradise, or the heavenly garden, is commonly confused with another order given this time to Adam, Eve, and Shayṭān to leave their earthly garden after Adam's temptation. If we carefully read the scene of the creation of Adam, which takes place in paradise, it is easy to see that the order to leave that place was an individual command given only to Iblīs. The order to the Devil (Iblīs) to leave paradise comes individually then and as solely addressed to him and doesn't include Adam and Eve as we read, "God said, 'Go away! Hell will be your reward, and the reward of any of them who follow you—an ample reward" (17:63). Likewise, all Qur'anic scenes referring to the Devil's (Iblīs's) dismissal from paradise share this individual tone of address, as we read, "Iblis said, 'I am better than him: You made me from fire, and him from clay.' 'Get out of here! You are rejected: My rejection will follow you till the Day of Judgement!'" (38:76–78). Also the same applies to, "God said, 'Iblis, why did you not bow down like the others?' and he answered, 'I will not bow to a mortal You created from dried clay, formed from dark mud,' 'Get out of here!' said God. 'You are an outcast, rejected until the Day of Judgement'" (15:32–34). What matters most is not to confuse what is depicted in all these scenes of individual dismissal, which solely address the Devil (Iblīs), with a plural dismissal from Adam's earthly garden that addresses this time not only the Devil (Shayṭān) but all who were involved in Adam's act of disobedience—which took place on earth—namely, Adam, Eve, and the Devil (Shayṭān). This is what we read, "He said, 'All of you get out! You are each other's enemies'" (7:24). Misinterpreting the *plural* dismissal of the Devil

(Shayṭān) we find in Q. 7:24 as repeating the *individual* dismissal of the Devil (*Iblīs*) from paradise should be reevaluated for a better understanding of the story.

(5) The Devil's immediate exile from paradise: Not only was the Devil individually dismissed from paradise, he was *immediately* dismissed after he refused to prostrate to Adam as well. This is what explains that the order was given to the Devil (Iblīs) as a single addressee in an event that predated anything Adam said or did. The Devil's act of disobedience and the consequences leading to his dismissal from the paradise are part of the story of creation and not to be confused with what will take place after the Devil is dismissed from paradise. According to the Qur'an, the Devil's (Iblīs's) disobedience immediately followed Adam's creation, "and the angels did so. But not Iblis: he refused to bow down like the others" (15:30–31). In addition, use of the conjunction *fa*–in 17:61, as we read, "When We said to the angels, 'Bow down before Adam,' [*fa*-] they all bowed down, but not Iblis" indicates a short time sequence between giving the order and the way the angels responded immediately to it. Next, immediately after the Devil (Iblīs) refused the order to prostrate he was exiled from paradise. This is clear from the *fa*-, which is used one more time to indicate a short time sequence, as we read, "God said, 'Iblis, why did you not bow down like the others?' and he answered, 'I will not bow to a mortal You created from dried clay, formed from dark mud.' [*fa*-] 'Get out of here!' said God" (15:32–34). The juxtaposition of these observations establishes the following about the story of the creation of Adam. The order was given to the angels and to the Devil (Iblīs) to prostrate to Adam the moment God breathes His spirit into him, allowing him by doing that to become His divine successor on earth. The angels immediately responded by prostrating unlike the Devil (Iblīs), who refused and protested against that divine choice. The Devil (Iblīs) was then immediately ordered to leave paradise. What followed the Devil's (Iblīs's) individual dismissal from paradise was his overt challenge in retaliation for his dismissal by causing Adam and his offspring to end up facing the same punishment, which is the eternal hell. This we find in, "'I will certainly take my due share of Your servants; I will mislead them and incite vain desires in them; I will command them to slit the ears of cattle; I will command them to tamper with God's creation. Whoever choses Satan as a patron instead of God is utterly ruined'" (4:118–19). Also we find the same meaning in, "Iblis said, 'I swear by Your might! I will tempt all but Your chosen servants'" (38:82). The plan of misleading and tempting Adam that the Devil (Iblīs) announces will take place once Adam starts his earthly journey in his earthly dwelling, the earthly garden given to him by God as his first residence.

The overt linguistic evidence I have mentioned for the Devil's (Iblīs's) immediate exile from paradise, which took place immediately after his refusal to prostrate to Adam the moment he was created, leaves no room to support the traditional argument for a series of subsequent events that took place in paradise after Adam was created and before he was allegedly dismissed from it. Even if we accept for the sake of argument that Adam, who was created in paradise, dwelled there for a while before he was dismissed, it will still be problematic to explain what happened between him and the Devil, who was already dismissed from paradise the same moment Adam was created! Ibn Qayyim mentions this difficulty as one of the reasons that caused some to argue for Adam's first dwelling as an earthly garden, "had that garden been above the heavens Satan would have never been able to ascend to it after he was brought down."[89] Al-Rāzī also mentioned different attempts made by exegetes to overcome this difficulty.[90] Some suggested that the Devil entered paradise after the serpent accepted to help him by swallowing him. "When the serpent entered paradise Satan came out of its mouth."[91] Others suggested that the Devil entered paradise disguised as an animal. Some said that Adam and Eve used to meet the Devil at heaven's door. Another opinion claims that the Devil seduced both Adam and Eve while he was on earth and they were in paradise. The vicissitude of the previous commentary fails to stay faithful to what can be truly described as scriptural. Therefore, and in an attempt to come up with better solutions, some—like Ibn ʿĀshūr explains—suggested two exiles of the Devil: while the first was addressed to the Devil solely when he refused to prostrate for Adam, "the second exile"[92] was addressed to the Devil, Adam, and Eve after the disobedience took place. While the first exile of the Devil still allowed him to enter paradise—mainly to enable seduction—the second exile banned him from entering paradise. Like Ibn ʿĀshūr, who dismissed this view, I concur, first for it being external to the Qur'anic text, which never makes any reference to two exiles, and second, for the contradiction entailed in dismissing the Devil from paradise and then allowing him temporarily to return only to enable him to seduce Adam and his wife! Contrary to this unsupported assumption, God, as the Qur'an confirms, didn't facilitate the disobedience to take place but warns Adam and Eve from the Devil's seduction[93] as we read in Q. 20:117. As far as I can see, the problem of what allowed the Devil to allegedly reenter paradise remains one of the unresolvable challenges that the traditional account of the story cannot really reconcile. This gap in the traditional story is another reason to support my argument for an immediate dismissal of the Devil from paradise and proposes that all of the subsequent events took place on earth and not in paradise.

(6) The indication of using the verb *waswasa*: It is important to note that all scenes referring to Adam in his first earthly dwelling use a specific verb for the act of seduction that resulted in his disobedience. This verb is *waswasa*,

which can be loosely translated as "to whisper" but can be proven to have a specific Qur'anic usage as well. As Goran Larsson (b. 1970) explains, "It is clear that whispering is associated above all with Satan, who by his whispering has the power to seduce men and women, leading them down the broad path that will take them to hell and damnation."[94]

In the Qur'an we find the verb used in the following verses, which describe Adam and Eve in their earthly dwelling. It can be even used to distinguish which Qur'anic passages refer to what happened on earth from those that describe events in paradise. First, we encounter the verb in, "But Satan whispered (*waswasa*) to Adam, saying, 'Adam, shall I show you the tree of immortality and power that never decays?'" (20:120), and second in, "Satan whispered (*waswasa*) to them so as to expose their nakedness which had been hidden from them: he said, 'Your Lord only forbade you the tree to prevent you becoming angels or immortals,' and he swore to them, 'I am giving you sincere advice'—he lured them with lies" (7:20–22). The same verb comes in a third place in the Qur'an to refer to the inner self-talk as we read, "We created man—We know what his soul whispers (*waswasa*) to him" (50:16). The meaning of *waswasa* as a Qur'anic term supports my understanding of the seduction as an earthly event, because the specific Qur'anic verb refers to a unique type of communication with a concealed reality. As we find in the three Qur'anic verses just cited, *waswasa* refers to an inner voice—talk and Satanic communication—when on earth and after Iblīs descended as Shayṭān. This specific usage of *waswasa* fits the concealed nature of Satan when on earth, who as the Qur'an asserts remains unseen by humans, "he and his forces can see you from where you cannot see them" (7:27).

(7) The meaning of *ihbiṭū* in Adam's exile order: The reinvestigation of the term the Qur'an uses to command Adam and Eve to leave their earthly garden reveals more about what had happened. The command *ihbiṭū* is usually misinterpreted as a command to "get down from a higher to a lower level."[95] This interpretation allows for a meaning more compatible with the idea of getting down from the heavens to earth. However, the way the same verb is used in another verse in the Qur'an suggests that this command is used in the Qur'an to mean "go" and not "get down." In 2:61 we read, "'Go (*ihbiṭū*) to Egypt and there you will find what you have asked for.'" In our case, in 2:35–36, we find the same verb used to order Adam and Eve to leave their earthly garden, "But Satan made them slip, and removed them from the state they were in. We said, 'Get out, (*ihbiṭū*) all of you! You are each other's enemy.'" As al-Māturīdī explains, both meanings are plausible.[96]

(8) The meaning of Adam and Eve's nakedness: The linguistic investigation of the consequence of eating from the tree can unearth more missing details. According to the Qur'anic text once Adam and Eve ate from the tree "their nakedness became exposed to them" (7:22). The careful use of

the verb *badā*, which means "to appear," as a reference to what happened means that Adam and Eve were naked, or, put differently, they were already naked. Eating from the tree didn't do anything but create a feeling of shame, guilt, and even humiliation. While they "began to put together leaves from the Garden to cover themselves" (7:22), Satan tried to humiliate them even more by "stripping them of their garments to expose their nakedness to them" (7:27). The fact that Adam and Eve had already possessed private parts, or sexual organs, even before they sinned indicates that they were already biologically prepared for an earthly journey including sexual reproduction. As mentioned before, al-Shaʿrāwī—in an attempt to respond to similar difficulties in the traditional narrative—argued for a garden in which Adam and Eve dwelled temporarily before they finally started their journey on earth after sinning. While al-Shaʿrāwī doesn't provide much elaboration on that garden, he describes the place as a garden where the first couple were divinely provided the nutrition they need. In that intermediate garden, as he argues, "the couple didn't have annoying stools or flatulent colic and they didn't have any health problems."[97] Their private parts were "mere similar holes."[98] I reject al-Shaʿrāwī's insertion of this intermediate status, first, for lacking any Qur'anic textual support and second, due to its overt contradiction with how nakedness was described, "their nakedness became exposed to them" (7:22). Adam and Eve as the Qur'an confirms were created naked. Their earthly sin only made them realize their nakedness.

(9) The addressees switch at the end of the "first test" story: Stories are told in the Qur'an for one reason. This reason is explained in "Tell them the stories[99] so that they may reflect" (7:176). This applies to Adam's story, which I refer to as the "first test." The story is followed by a switch in the addressee that takes place immediately after the exile of Adam and Eve from their earthly garden. This switch addresses the children of Adam: "Children of Adam, We have given you garments to cover your nakedness and as adornment for you; the garment of God-consciousness is the best of all garments—this is one of God's signs, so that people may take heed. [27] Children of Adam, do not let Satan seduce you, as he did your parents, causing them to leave the Garden, stripping them of their garments to expose their nakedness to them" (7:26–27).

This switch in addressee, which includes the children of Adam as the targeted audience, is another assurance that the act of disobedience took place in earth and not in heaven. In addition, the clear reference to Adam and Eve in the previous verse as "your parents" assets that the biological reproduction plan was already in place when Adam sinned. The traditional account, which claims that Adam was not originally designed to live on earth, cannot explain this immediate reference to the children of Adam in the midst of a story that allegedly took place in paradise.

Contrary to the traditional understanding of the story of the first disobedience, the story is told not to ignite feelings of guilt and human unworthiness, but to assure the divine status of Adam's offspring. The journey was intended from the beginning to be earthly. Humans were not designed to live in heaven, and Adam didn't really lose his right to live in paradise due to one sin he committed. Adam, very shortly after starting his earthly journey, committed a sin by disobeying God, but then he was instructed on how to repent and he was forgiven and blessed. The story is told to give a message of hope to Adam's children, who, like their father, will keep sinning but can still be forgiven and blessed as long as they repent to God the way their father repented. The divine status as God's deputies was not lost due to Adam's one sin. Rather, the lesson was a lesson on how to keep the divine status active by way of repenting and going back to God's path every time one deviates from it. The immediate switch of the addressee to the children of Adam after the story is shared supports my argument for Adam's exile of his earthly garden as a first test.

(10) Compatibility with other Qur'anic stories: The story of Adam's disobedience when adequately understood is like the story of Moses, Jesus, Abraham, Job, and all other prophets. The story is told for the purpose of learning. Nothing in any of those Qur'anic stories is supposed to be equally applicable to anyone other than those mentioned. Adam was warned not to eat from one tree. All consequences of obeying or disobeying God are limited to Adam and can't be equally applicable to his offspring, the same way nothing in the stories of Moses, Jesus, Job, and so on can be equally applicable to others. The fact that Adam is the father of humanity doesn't and shouldn't allow for exceptions like those encountered in the traditional account of the story; that is, in allowing the burden of his sin to transfer to his offspring. The Qur'anic story was specific and accurate and addressed Adam by concrete individual and personal consequences that would apply to him for disobeying God, "so We said, 'Adam, this is your enemy, yours and your wife's; do not let him drive you out of the garden and make you miserable. In the garden you will never go hungry, feel naked, be thirsty, or suffer the heat of the sun'" (20:117–18). This dialogue—exclusively addressed to Adam and his wife—does not include Adam's offspring in consequence. Any attempt to include Adam's offspring in the exile's outcomes is foreign to what is confirmed in the Qur'an. It is important to remember that Adam's test is individual as well as all its related consequences. The earthly garden that Adam was dismissed from was not granted to all humankind, but was individual, prepared as the first dwelling solely for Adam and his wife. Other than learning a lesson from the story, Adam's offspring are not implicated therein. This conclusion matches the linguistic observation from addressing only Adam and Eve with

the command and the explanation of the consequences of disobeying it. Also, this fits more with the Qur'anic shared style of prophetic narratives, such that understanding Adam's story as a test fits a reoccurring Qur'anic theme that acknowledges testing as an essential part of human life including prophets. Finally, as I mentioned before, this interpretation is more consistent with the Qur'anic sense of justice where no one individual can be held accountable for others' choices.[100]

## CONCLUSION: THE RECONSTRUCTION OF THE QUR'ANIC STORY OF ADAM AND EVE

As previously discussed, what I refer to as the "story of creation" is commonly confused with what I call the "first test." To explain more, the second story starts from where the first one ends, with the Devil's dismissal from paradise. This part of the story is commonly misunderstood when added to what happened when Adam was created in paradise. For reasons previously discussed, all subsequent events immediately following the Devil's dismissal don't take place in paradise but on earth. To be more specific, they take place in an earthly garden that God prepared as the first dwelling for Adam and his wife, Eve. Unlike al-Shaʿrāwī, who clearly rejects Adam's exile from paradise but instead introduces a loose concept of a "beautiful garden"[101] and "a place"[102] in which Adam and Eve were provided all idyllic necessities of life, and in which they temporarily lived in before they "ascended to earth to start the succession assignment,"[103] I hold that dwelling to be earthly. As we have seen, after God announced in heaven His intention to send a divine deputy to earth, a dialogue between God and the angels took place concerning Adam as the best candidate for such an honor; however, Iblīs—unlike the angels—took one step further by objecting to the divine decision and by refusing to submit to God's choice by prostrating to Adam. Furthermore, Iblīs announced his enmity to Adam and his offspring and his plan to tempt them. The Qur'anic scene then shifts to Adam's earthly journey in a garden prepared for him as his first dwelling on earth. This scene, unlike what the traditional narrative claims, takes place on earth, not in paradise. In addition, that garden was a garden prepared solely for Adam and his wife as their first dwelling. It is not a reference to better conditions for life that were granted to all humans. Adam lost his right to one specific garden he was promised. He didn't cause all his offspring to lose the chance to live and enjoy ideal conditions of life that humans were allegedly promised. This part of the story is told like all other Qur'anic stories for a moral lesson to be taken away—which I explain in detail. According to the Qur'anic story, Adam started his earthly journey in a garden. In that garden Adam was provided ideal conditions of life. The following verse individually addresses Adam with the offer, without including his offspring, "In the garden you will never go hungry, feel naked, be thirsty, or suffer the heat of the sun'" (20:118–19). However, in that earthly garden Adam had to learn his first lesson—a lesson that constitutes the core of human divine assignment on earth. Adam was tested, the same way all humans are tested. For Adam, as it will be the case for his offspring, testing provides an opportunity to prove divine merit as "God's gods" on earth. His first test started by an order not to approach one tree out of all other trees in the garden. Also, he was warned that the Devil, who is referred to as Shayṭān at this time, will do his best to make him disobey God. Shayṭān, who had already announced his enmity to Adam and his offspring the moment he was dismissed from paradise, manages to tempt Adam and Eve to disobey God by eating from the forbidden tree. The scene eventually ends with their repentance and with God's forgiveness, but more importantly, the scene ends with a message not to Adam this time but to his offspring to learn a lesson from what happened to their parents.

A big lesson the story communicates is the following: the focal point of religious commitment is based on love, trust, and obedience. When Adam was prohibited from eating from one tree what mattered is his obedience; furthermore, what matters most in our case is the lesson we can learn from the way we should react after sinning. The fact that the Qur'anic command didn't specify the tree by anything other than it being a mere tree suggests that the prohibition itself was of central importance. The tree was probably an ordinary tree. What mattered was not the tree itself as much as the lesson Adam was supposed to learn; which is the submission to what God orders. Wadud describes the tree as a mere "symbol of the test."[104] Adam sinned but then he repented and God accepted his repentance. This summarizes the story and the reason the story is told as a Qur'anic story in the first place. The reason the Qur'an dismissed describing the tree as unique is because the tree was not unique or special. The evidence is the fact that nothing happened when both Adam and Eve ate from the tree.[105] All what befell Adam and his wife on earth was, then, a test. In this book, I move now from highlighting Adam's test to highlighting test as the core of human divine assignment on earth.

## NOTES

1. I am loosely using the term "Devil" for a distinction I will shortly introduce between two Qur'anic terms: Iblīs and Shayṭān.

2. Gabriel Said Reynolds, "Biblical Background," in *The Wiley Blackwell Companion to the Qur'an*, ed. Andrew Rippin and Jawid Mojaddedi (Chichester, UK: Wiley-Blackwell, 2017), 304.

3. Burhān al-Dīn al-Biqā'ī, *Naẓm al-durar* (Cairo: Dār al-Kitāb al-Islāmī, 1984), 1:284.
4. 'Abd Allāh Ibn 'Abbās, *Tanwīr al-miqbās min tafsīr Ibn 'Abbās* (Beirut: Dār al-Kutub al-'Ilmiyya, 1992), 9.
5. Ismā'īl b. 'Umar Ibn Kathīr, *al-Bidāya wa-l-nihāya* (Beirut: Dār al-Ma'ārif, 1990), 1:75.
6. Abū Manṣūr al-Māturīdī, *Tāwīlāt al-Qur'ān* (Istanbul: Dār al-Mīzān, 2005), 1:89.
7. Rashīd Riḍā, *Tafsīr al-manār* (Egypt: Dār al-Manār, 1947), 1:277.
8. Ibid.
9. Abū 'Abd Allāh b. Abī Bakr b. Ayyūb Ibn Qayyim al-Jawziyya, *Ḥādī al-arwāḥ ilā bilād al-afrāḥ* (Jeddah: Dār 'Ālam al-Fu'ād, 2007), 50.
10. Riḍā, *Tafsīr al-manār*, 1:277.
11. Ibn Qayyim al-Jawziyya, *Ḥādī al-arwāḥ*, 50; Fakhr al-Dīn Muḥammad b. 'Umar al-Rāzī, *al-Tafsīr al-kabīr* (Beirut: Dār al-Fikr, 1981), 2:3.
12. 'Alī b. Ibrāhīm al-Qummī, *Tafsīr 'Alī ibn Ibrāhīm al-Qummī* (Qom: Mu'assasat al-Imām al-Mahdī, 2014), 1:71.
13. Muḥammad Mutwallī al-Sha'rāwī, *Tafsīr al-Sha'rāwī* (Cairo: Akhbār al-Yawm, 1991), 260.
14. Ibid., 258.
15. See Shahrour, al-Qasas al-Qur'aani, Qira'at Mu'aasira, Vol. 1, Dar al-Saqi, 2010, page 320. I am grateful to an anonymous reviewer for suggesting this valuable reference.
16. Ibn Kathīr, *al-Bidāya wa-l-nihāya*, 1:71.
17. al-Rāzī, *al-Tafsīr al-kabīr*, 2:181.
18. Ibn Kathīr, *al-Bidāya wa-l-nihāya*, 1:70.
19. Ruthven, *Islam*, 26.
20. Muḥammad Ḥusayn al-Ṭabāṭabā'ī, *al-Mīzān* (Beirut: al-A'lamī, 1997), 1:117.
21. Barbara Stowasser, *Women in the Qur'an, Traditions, and Interpretation* (New York: Oxford University Press, 1994), 27.
22. Maḥmūd b. 'Umar al-Zamakhsharī, *al-Kashshāf* (Beirut: Dār al-Ma'rifa, 2009), 70.
23. Everything I assert about Adam should be understood as equally applicable to both Adam and Eve. The investigation of the lost gender egalitarian message of the story of creation is a project that I extensively discuss in Hasan, *Decoding the Egalitarianism of the Qur'an*.
24. al-Sha'rāwī, *Tafsīr al-Sha'rāwī*, 260.
25. Amina Wadud, *The Qur'an and Women* (New York: Oxford University Press, 1999), 23.
26. While I stress in the first point Adam's role as a successor, I stress here the existence of earth, which predated Adam's creation.
27. Ibn 'Abbās, *Tanwīr al-miqbās*, 277–78.
28. Ibid., 8.
29. Ismā'īl b. 'Umar Ibn Kathīr, *Tafsīr al-Qur'ān al-'aẓīm* (Riyadh: Dār Ṭayyiba, 1999), 1:213.

30. ʿAbd al-Qādīr Shībah al-Ḥamd, *Tahdhīb al-tafsīr wa-tajrid al-taʾwīl* (Riyadh: Muʾassasat ʿUlūm al-Qurʾān, 2011), 1:105.

31. Muḥammad b. Aḥmad al-Qurṭubī, *al-Jāmiʿ li-aḥkām al-Qurʾān* (Beirut: al-Risāla, 2006), 1:451.

32. I mean as a human dwelling. As I argue in detail later, Adam was created in heaven, but that heaven was not intended nor designed to be his initial dwelling. Heaven as a human dwelling is the eternal heaven prepared as a reward for the righteous.

33. ʿAbd al-Ṣabūr Shāhīn, *Abī Ādam* (Cairo: Akhbār al-Yawm, 1900), 133.

34. Please see the next section on reconstructing the story for the full Qur'anic argument.

35. al-Qurṭubī, *al-Jāmiʿ li-aḥkām al-Qurʾān*, 1:476.

36. Ibid.

37. ʿUkāsha ʿAbd al-Mannān al-Ṭībī, *al-Shāyṭān fī ẓilāl al-Qurʾān li-Shaykh Sayyid Quṭb* (Cairo: Maktabat al-Turāth al-Islāmī, 1992), 13.

38. Ibn Qayyim al-Jawziyya, *Ḥādī al-arwāḥ*, 48.

39. al-Qurṭubī, *al-Jāmiʿ li-aḥkām al-Qurʾān*, 1:451.

40. al-Biqāʿī, *Naẓm al-durar*, 1:287.

41. Ramzī Naʿnāʿa, *al-Isrāʾīliyyāt wa-atharuhā fī kutub al-tafsir* (Damascus: Dār al-Qalam; Beirut: Dār al-Ḍiyāʾ, 1970), 23.

42. The image of Eve as the conspirer is only one way in which the Qur'anic story was exegetically reshaped. However, here I move from discussing Eve's alleged image to reconstructing the whole story. For more on Eve's role, see Hasan, *Decoding the Egalitarianism of the Qur'an*.

43. ʿAbd al-Raḥmān b. al-Kamāl al-Suyūṭī, *al-Durr al-manthūr* (Cairo: Markaz Ḥajar, 2003), 10:253.

44. Hasan, *Decoding the Egalitarianism of the Qur'an*, 8.

45. Muḥammad al-Bukhārī, *Ṣaḥīḥ al-Bukhārī* (Damascus: Dār Ibn Kathīr, 2002), 1639 (hadith no. 6614).

46. Hasan, *Decoding the Egalitarianism of the Qur'an*, 11.

47. Roberto Tottoli, "Narrative Literature," in *The Wiley Blackwell Companion to the Qur'an*, 564.

48. Jane Dammen McAuliffe, "Introduction," in *The Cambridge Companion to the Qurʾān*, ed. Jane Dammen McAuliffe (Cambridge and New York: Cambridge University Press, 2007), 5.

49. Hasan, *Decoding the Egalitarianism of the Qur'an*, 17.

50. Muḥammad b. al-Ṭāhir Ibn ʿĀshūr, *al-Taḥrīr wa-l-tanwīr* (Tunis: al-Dār al-Tūnisiyya, 1984), 1:430.

51. Taqī al-Dīn Aḥmad b. ʿAbd al-Ḥalīm Ibn Taymiyya, *Majmūʿ al-fatāwā* (Medina: Majmaʿ al-Malik Fahd li-Tibāʿa al-Muṣḥaf al-Sharīf, 2004), 4:347.

52. al-Ṭabāṭabāʾī, *al-Mīzān*, 1:140.

53. Hasan, *Decoding the Egalitarianism of the Qur'an*, 15.

54. By limiting my argument to Adam, I am not indicating any ontological prioritization of the creation of Adam, which I have previously argued against. This is only to simplify the argument. All of what applies to Adam applies to Eve. Eve, as I argued

before, was created along with Adam from one soul. Adam here stands for human, both male and female.

55. al-Zamakhsharī, *al-Kashshāf*, 70.
56. Ibn ʿĀshūr, *al-Taḥrīr wa-l-tanwīr*, 1:403.
57. ʿAbd al-Raḥmān al-Thaʿālibī, *al-Juzʾ al-awwal [al-rābiʿ] min Kitāb al-Jawāhir al-ḥisān fī tafsīr al-Qurʾān* (Algiers: A. B. M. al-Turkī, 1905), 1:43.
58. H. U. Weitbrecht, *The Teaching of the Qurʾān with an Account of Its Growth and a Subject Index* (New York: Macmillan Co, 1919), 39.
59. Riḍā, *Tafsīr al-manār*, 1:265.
60. Ibid.
61. The translator's choice here, "bow down," is not literal and doesn't address the core of the meaning.
62. Whitney S. Bodman, *The Poetics of Iblis: Narrative Theology in the Qur'an* (Cambridge, MA: Harvard University Press, 2011), 183.
63. Muḥammad Amīn al-Shanqīṭī, *Aḍwāʾ al-bayān* (Riyadh: Dār al-Faḍīla; Mansoura: Dār al-Hādī al-Nabawī, 2005), 43.
64. Committee of Scholars, *al-Tafsīr al-wasīṭ* (Medina: Maṭbaʿat al-Muṣḥaf al-Sharīf, 1992), 1:76.
65. Ibn Kathīr, *Tafsīr al-Qurʾān al-ʿaẓīm*, 1:223.
66. ʿAlī b. Muḥammad al-Māwardī, *al-Nukat wa-l-ʿuyūn* (Beirut: Dār al-Kutub al-ʿIlmiyya, 2010), 1:99.
67. Riḍā, *Tafsīr al-manār*, 1:262.
68. al-Shaʿrāwī, *Tafsīr al-Shaʿrāwī*, 246.
69. al-Shanqīṭī, *Aḍwāʾ al-bayān*, 43.
70. Barbara Stowasser, "Theodicy and the Many Meanings of Adam and Eve," in *Theodicy and Justice in Modern Islamic Thought: The Case of Said Nursi*, ed. Ibrahim M. Abu-Rabi (London: Routledge, 2016), 3.
71. al-Rāzī, *al-Tafsīr al-kabīr*, 2:192.
72. Ibid.
73. Ibid.
74. Noam Chomsky, *Language and Mind* (Cambridge: Cambridge University Press, 2006), 90.
75. Ibid., 112.
76. David Braun, "Empty Names, Fictional Names, Mythical Names," *NoÛs* 39 (2005): 596.
77. Mustafa Ozturk, "The Tragic Story of Iblis (Satan) in the Qur'an." *Journal of Islamic Research* 2, no 2 (2009): 143.
78. Ibn ʿĀshūr, *al-Taḥrīr wa-l-tanwīr*, 16:321.
79. Ibn ʿAbbās, *Tanwīr al-miqbās*, 5:321.
80. Bodman, *The Poetics of Iblis*, 18.
81. Ibid.
82. Ibid., 19.
83. Ibid., 20.
84. Ibid., 26.

85. Torsten Löfstedt, "The Creation and Fall of Adam: A Comparison of the Qur'anic and Biblical Accounts." *Swedish Missiological Themes* 93, no. 4 (2005): 467.

86. I don't accept this suggestion either, because it leaves behind the question of a similar analogy that should be highlighted—if the same logic is to be applied—between Adam, who like Iblīs was mentioned as a proper name in the story of creation, and his offspring. We don't draw a distinction between Adam and his offspring simply because of Adam's individual mention the same way we should not draw that type of distinction to resolve the problem caused by switching from Iblīs to Shayṭān.

87. The translation here does not match the Qur'anic text, which uses "Iblīs."

88. In the Qur'an nothing should or can be described as pointless or random. See Q. 1:11.

89. Ibn Qayyim al-Jawziyya, *Ḥādī al-arwāḥ*, 73.

90. al-Rāzī, *al-Tafsīr al-kabīr*, 2:16.

91. Ibid.

92. Ibn ʿĀshūr, *al-Taḥrīr wa-l-tanwīr*, 1:434.

93. Which is an earthly seduction.

94. Goran Larsson, "The Sound of Satan: Different Aspects of Whispering in Islamic theology." *Temenos* 48, no.1 (2012): 53.

95. al-Qurṭubī, *al-Jāmiʿ li-aḥkām al-Qurʾān*, 1:475.

96. al-Māturīdī, *Tāwīlāt al-Qurʾān*, 1:106.

97. al-Shaʿrāwī, *Tafsīr al-Shaʿrāwī*, 4080.

98. Ibid., 4083.

99. It appears in Abdel Haleem's translation in the singular form ("story"), while the original Arabic of the Qur'an has *qaṣaṣ* in the plural, as per my translation here.

100. Q. 35:18.

101. al-Shaʿrāwī, *Tafsīr al-Shaʿrāwī*, 4079.

102. Ibid.

103. Ibid., 4095.

104. Wadud, *The Qurʾan and Women*, 23.

105. Physically or biologically.

# *Chapter 2*

# The Divine Assignment

## *The Divine on Earth*

Adam was created from earth. More importantly, he was created for an earthly journey, as we have seen in chapter 1. He was entrusted the sacrosanct assignment of succeeding God on earth. In the first chapter I also highlighted a missing aspect of Adam's story, which should be understood as the first human test. Our earthly journey as a test, as I argue in this book, is the core of our existence. In addition, this understanding provides a key to unlocking theodicy as I discuss throughout the book as well. While in chapter 3 I explain individual and variable testing of humans, I argue in this chapter for the human divine assignment on earth, or what is known as religion, as the major divine responsibility and the ultimate test. The divine journey of humans on earth and the complete fulfillment of the assignment include many challenges. As I argue in this chapter, epistemic difficulties associated with human religiosity—which many detractors of religion cite as external anti-religious arguments—are in fact defining factors deeply woven in the same fabric of what religion as a divine test means.

The Qur'anic text confirms hardship as the core of the human earthly journey: "We have created man for toil and trial" (90:4). While the concept of hardship can be extended to include all earthly life-related difficulties and challenges, I focus here on one specific epistemic hardship, dealing with which can define us as God's successors on earth, namely, religion.

While religious skepticism might sound like an undesirable instance for the majority of faithful believers for obvious reasons, epistemic religious skepticism might be one option to consider if we wish to better understand religious thinking and keep a safe distance between the religious text and our understanding of it, more importantly, to keep a distance between the fixed, unchangeable, and unknown content of that text and our variable human approaches to religious reality. One thing to keep in mind: Our human approach to religious reality is fallible, diverse, and relative. It has always been like that and it will always continue to be.

In order to make any headway in understanding religion one essential assertion must be kept in mind: There is no real and tangible sense of definite, apodictic, and change-resistant epistemic religious knowledge that we can capture and arrest at any current moment. At best, there are epistemic speculations that not only can change as the thinking subjects (humans) change, but can also change within the same subject as he or she gains deeper insights, learns more, and so on. A reversed and less progressive change can also take place as we grow old, forget, or lose the interest we used to have, or as we lose the energy we need to pursue our old topics of interest. As much as this idea might sound uncomfortable, especially if we take into consideration our lazy mental habits as people, which keep nurturing the tendency to stop questioning and analyzing any belief once we or others we trust label it as "true," our discomfort should not stop the ongoing human effort to reinterpret the interpreted and keep an open mind.

Needless to say, what I mean by epistemic religious skepticism is not to be understood as the denial of the existence of God as an ontological reality; rather, what I mean here doesn't exceed the affirmation of the abiding need to rethink and reevaluate religious reality as conceptualized by our human faculties. In other words, my argument doesn't exceed the acknowledgment that while ontological religious reality can exist, there is no guarantee that our temporal epistemic pinpointing or identification of the fluidity of that reality (necessarily) corresponds to its original ontological status.

The challenge of concealed religious reality is at the core of our test as human beings, because making sound choices while provided nothing but general divine guidance is the ultimate success of humans as God's deputies on earth. In the following, I provide Qur'an-based core challenges that define human religiosity as a test. As mentioned before, while these elements are commonly cited and used to challenge the same concept of being religious, and even to undermine religion itself, I argue for these elements as essential factors in understanding what does religion as a test stand for.

(1) Religious thinking is metaphysical by definition: Interestingly enough, in the Qur'an, true believers are described as those who "believe in the unseen" (2:2) and those who "believe in the revelation sent down to you and what was sent before you" (2:4). True believers are not praised for "knowing" the unseen or what has been revealed, a goal that no one should claim, unless one is either too arrogant or ignorant to do so; rather, they are praised for "believing" in both. It might be relevant also to remember that, at least from a Qur'anic point of view, "for certain" (102:5) religious knowledge or belief, or what we might call based on experience belief, doesn't come until "the end" (102:4) and after "you go into your graves" (102:2). This is

because concealing religious reality is what makes humans' earthly journey a real opportunity to prove their merit as gods on earth. Had religious reality—including God Himself—been simply revealed, religious commitment, devotion, and even the concept of religion itself would have been superfluous and redundant. The recognition of the insensibility of the human religious experience of the divine is more observable in the monotheistic traditions, but can apply as well to all religions and is observed in the history of human religions and their endless attempts to unlock the mysteriousness of the unseen. It is true that "what religions attempt to approach may be considered beyond human utterance. Believers build statues and buildings through which to worship the divine, but these forms are not the divine itself. Because people are addressing the invisible, it can be suggested only through metaphor."[1]

Concealing religious reality as a condition for the worldly test and for the fulfilment of the human divine assignment on earth is reportedly confirmed in the Qur'an. We read about the impossibility of any sensible experience of God as an eternal worldly law: "No vision can take Him in, but He takes in all vision" (6:103). The previous verse does not allow exceptions as it is literally mentioned and unequivocally affirmed here and in other places in the Qur'an. Likewise we read, "It is not granted to any mortal that God should speak to him except through revelation or from behind a veil, or by sending a messenger to reveal by His command what He will: He is exalted and wise" (42:51). Concealing religious reality as an essential condition for our experience of religion to be considered sound and merit-worthy is the reason "God didn't allow Moses to see Him in this world."[2] It is the reason Moses even had to repent from making a request to see God as we read: "When Moses came for Our appointment, and his Lord spoke to him, he said, 'My Lord, show Yourself to me: let me see You!' He said, 'You will never see Me, but look at that mountain: if it remains standing firm, you will see Me,' and when his Lord revealed Himself to the mountain, He made it crumble: Moses fell down unconscious. When he recovered, he said, 'Glory be to You! To You I turn in repentance! I am the first to believe!'" (7:143). But more importantly, the Qur'an announces clearly that no religious reality can or will be revealed before the end of this worldly life, as we know it, in a clear affirmation of concealing this reality as a condition to the continuity of the human assignment on earth, "Those who do not fear to meet Us say, 'Why are the angels not sent down to us?' or 'Why can we not see our Lord?' They are too proud of themselves and too insolent. There will be no good news for the guilty on the Day they see the angels. The angels will say, 'You cannot cross the forbidden barrier,' and We shall turn to the deeds they have done and scatter them like dust" (25:21–23). According to the mainstream Sunni consensus, "God cannot be seen in the worldly life."[3] The visual experience of God is viewed as "the noblest, the most great, the most glorified, the most blessed out of all heaven's blessings."[4] The impossibility of having any sensible experience of God in the worldly life[5] is also extended by the majority of Muslim theologians to include the impossibility of knowing God per se. The Qur'an describes God as a being beyond comparison and analogy, "There is nothing like Him" (42:11) and even as an existence beyond human comprehension, "He knows what is before and behind them, though they do not comprehend Him" (20:110). "This does not contradict the belief in His existence,"[6] but assures divine transcendentalism as a core Islamic theological belief.

(2) Religious thinking is unempirical by definition: The relative nature of religious beliefs makes them better to be compared to historical beliefs than to scientific beliefs. One basic character of "reality" is to give us better options to deal with the world according to what we adopt as real and what we dismiss as false. For example, knowing that the cup of coffee I am about to drink is hot can give me better options so as not to burn my tongue as I take my first sip. In other words, adopting or neglecting scientific beliefs comes with immediate empirical outcomes and consequences, both good and bad. This is not the same, however, for religious beliefs, because adopting or abandoning a certain religious belief can't be empirically proven to bring about the same set of easily observable consequences. People can live fulfilling lives as believers, atheists, polytheists, infidels, agnostics, and so on, regardless of what they believe in and without a concrete change in the quality of their lives, what happens to them, and what doesn't happen to them.

I have started by comparing religious beliefs to historical beliefs. Our comprehension of religious reality is best compared to our knowledge of history. As much as it might sound entertaining and satisfactory to think of, one monolithic concept of history that corresponds to our belief of what must have happened; no epistemic guarantee of any kind can assure us that our belief of what had happened is a matching copy of what had really happened. Because there will always be a gap between what had happened and what had been witnessed, narrated, written, documented, told, and even what has been fabricated about what had happened. Our historical beliefs are always to be contrasted and challenged by others' historical beliefs inasmuch as our religious beliefs can always be challenged by others' religious beliefs, despite the fact that underlying both cases in the analogy there exists one real history and one ontological religious reality. "History is written by the victors" is often-cited but rarely thoroughly evaluated. To appreciate how irrelevant our beliefs might be, of what had happened, let us imagine the following radical case. What if we wake up tomorrow to realize that all what we have been told about human history was wrong? Let's imagine that universal answers we have hitherto received as fact—who built the pyramids, who invented the light bulb, who used the term "democracy" first, and so on—are all mixed up and wrong. In fact, beyond feelings of ignorance and stupidity nothing will change the way we will live the rest of our day.

(3) Religious thinking is unrewardable by definition: In addition to the absence of empirical proof, religious thinking is also challenged by the apparent lack of religious-based psychological reinforcement. The absence of any direct experiential worldly consequence of adopting or abandoning a certain religious belief is an essential part of understanding the divine test as an epistemic hardship. As the Qur'an confirms, no immediate worldly outcomes are essentially caused by what we believe in and what we do not:

> If anyone desires [only] the fleeting life, We speed up whatever We will in it, for whoever We wish; in the end We have prepared Hell for him in which to burn, disgraced and rejected. But if anyone desires the life to come and strives towards it as he should, as a true believer, his striving will be thanked. To both the latter and the former, We give some of your Lord's bounty. [Prophet], your Lord's bounty is not restricted—see how We have given some more than others—but the Hereafter holds greater ranks and greater favors. (17:18–21)

Had there been immediate outcomes and consequences that follow our religious commitment or negligence, or even our religious indifference, we would have all our religious experience nullified. If humans were guided by an immediately rewarding religious experience that promptly and spontaneously ends by rewarding the adoption of sound religious beliefs—whatever those beliefs might be—and punishing the adoption of false beliefs, the core of the religious experience as a worldly test would be jeopardized. The enhancement of behavior and the stimulation of specific outcomes by providing immediate rewards and punishments is a test even animals can pass—as psychological testing of animals confirms.[7] This is not the kind of test, however, the entrusted deputy of God on earth was given. Rather, the worldly test essentially includes an epistemic hardship by way of removing any clues, either based on immediate or even long-term rewards or punishments.

(4) Religious thinking is variable by definition: The assertion of religion as an epistemic hardship and affirming the irreplaceability of epistemic religious skepticism, which should always lead us while interpreting the divine text, any divine text, doesn't only match the fallibility of the cognitive abilities of the thinking subjects, "humans," and the invisible nature of the thinking object—in our case, "the unseen"—but also reflects more authentically the pluralism of religious beliefs. Diverse religious beliefs can be equally logically affirmed, can coexist, and can equally survive exclusivism. Since the dawn of history, people have adopted different, variable, and many times antithetical religious beliefs that have all survived the test of time and functionality regardless of their variety. The fact that religious thinking can be as

diverse as humans affirms religion as a test, a challenge, and an epistemic hardship. All religious beliefs, good and bad—if any can be described this way—have in principle the capability of standing the test of time and merit. Those who adopt religious beliefs different from our own do not owe us an explanation inasmuch as we do not owe them an explanation for denying what they sincerely believe in. The acknowledgment of the variety of religious beliefs is an assurance of the absence of a monolithic sense of one final and definite epistemic religious reality. The Qur'an makes a subtle reference to this diversity of beliefs as a fact. "This is your community, one community—and I am your Lord: be mindful of Me—but they have split their community into sects, each rejoicing in their own" (23:52–53). The Qur'anic acknowledgment of the diversity of episteme religious knowledge as a predetermined divine plan supports the argument for religious pluralism as a decreed and an ongoing human experience of God, "We have assigned a law and a path to each of you. If God had so willed, He would have made you one community, but He wanted to test you through that which He has given you, so race to do good: you will all return to God and He will make clear to you the matters you differed about" (5:48). These different, and sometimes contradicting, human understandings might all claim a firsthand approach to the transcendental monolithic divine meaning. Another serious concern that is no less complicated and divergent than the previous one stems from the different ways in which various cultures reinterpret, reshape, and even reproduce the same religion. Joseph Camilleri and Sven Schottmann rightly observe this deep cultural/religious entanglement:

> Both religion and culture are all-encompassing concepts that cannot be easily or usefully categorized by making one the subset of the other, or by attempting to reduce one to the realm of the sacred and assigning the other to the realm of the profane. Nor is it satisfactory to characterize religion in terms of doctrinal or metaphysical claims on the one hand, and culture purely in relation to ethnicity or "primordial" attachments on the other. Both culture and religion delineate in complex and interacting ways the boundaries that separate the insider from the outsider, the internal from the external, right from wrong or at least acceptable from reprehensible conduct. There is nevertheless a distinctive quality to religion, which has to do with an enduring yearning for some form of transcendence, whether expressed by belief in God or more amorphous but no less potent cosmic notions that take the human being beyond the reality of the physical universe. Religion is inseparable from culture in that all religions, in different ways and to different degrees, entail stories, myths, rituals and ethical precepts, which are themselves important building blocks of culture. Yet the culture of any society is necessarily multilayered, and seldom the pure reflection of the beliefs and practices of any one religion or even combination of religions. Culture, which includes language, technology, institutions and much else, is

best understood as a complex mosaic to which different epochs and population movements contribute different ways of knowing, perceiving, feeling and living in the world as societies seek to adapt to the challenges of a ceaselessly changing environment.[8]

(5) Religious thinking is finite by definition: The assertion that the perfect intellectual unfolding of religious reality is not a project that can be humanly accomplished and arrested in time and place is more compatible with a Qur'anic confirmation; namely, that absolute religious knowledge is a sanctified divine privilege preserved for God, who alone can soundly claim it, as we read, "He knows what is not seen as well as what is seen" (13:9). The Qur'anic text affirms hiding religious reality as a worldly law and norm that allows only knowledge communicated via revelation through messengers and prophets, "God would not show you [people] what is hidden; God chooses as His messengers whoever He will. So believe in God and His messengers" (3:179). Main core concepts in any religion can remain ambiguous even for the most faithful believers. The textual support from the Qur'an asserts the impossibility of knowing God per se or His attributes. "You have only been given a little knowledge" (17:85), especially when this knowledge deals with the unseen, "So I swear by what you can see and by what you cannot see" (69:38–39). Ibn Taymiyya summarizes the Sunni theological consensus that survived a long history of *kalām* debates by saying, "the reference of His names and attributes is a reality known only to Him."[9] Even in the Sufi tradition—which holds personalizing the experience of the Divine as its most lofty goal—the claim of knowing God per se remains a far-fetched hope. Jalāl al-Dīn Rūmī (1207–1273) says:

> If you have musk in a container with a narrow neck, you put your finger into it. You can't get the musk, but your finger is perfumed nonetheless and your sense of smell is gratified. Being mindful of God is like this. Although you cannot reach His essence, remembrance of Him has many effects, and many great benefits accrue.[10]

The impossibility of knowing God's attributes refers to what is already confirmed about God in the Qur'an; reverting to what is textually supported was thereby a way to end a long tradition of debating this subject by major *kalām* schools. The difficulty is reconciled only by way of "confirming divine attributes the way they were mentioned,"[11] and denying what has been textually denied or omitted. The first category of affirmed divine attributes of God includes, but is not limited to, knowledge, life, hearing, seeing, and so on. The second category of denied divine attributes includes, but is not limited to, ignorance, injustice, sleeping, and so on.

Now, a very popular argument against the existence of God, or any religious belief, uses the fact that God doesn't physically and tangibly exist as an object of experiential human knowledge. This argument ignores that *believing* in a nonphysical God, or put differently, believing in God as an incomprehensible existent, lies at the core of the human religious experience. Had God been seen, heard, and concretely known, all religious commitment would have turned areligious, because this approachability suffices to end all and every "epistemic hardship."

(6) Religious thinking is subjective by definition: Supernatural and spiritual, including religious, beliefs are in their majority faith-driven beliefs and not proof-driven. This claim is true even for those who adopt a more scientific approach to religion. Ideally speaking, hypotheses—including religious hypotheses—are not treated as proven theories unless supported by evidence, data collection, information assessment, and even intellectual analysis. However, all of the above in case of religious beliefs are usually partially used for the advantage of supporting already adopted beliefs, not for the purpose of testing or assessing them. For the devout believer, counterexamples are commonly treated as trivialities. Even people providing contrary testimonies are commonly treated either as charlatan outsiders who need to be confronted, or as errant fellows who need to be guided. Bryan Caplan (b. 1971) says, "We habitually tune out unwanted information on subjects we don't care about. In the same vein, I claim that we turn off our rational faculties on subjects where we don't care about the truth."[12] Even the occurrence of something as compelling as a miracle cannot provide much help at the end of the day. For the nonbeliever miracles can be simply and easily dismissed as magic tricks or hallucinations. The Qur'an asserts that miracles don't speak to those who actively choose to deny them:

> They swear by God with their most solemn oaths that if a miraculous sign came to them they would believe in it. Say [Prophet], "Signs are in the power of God alone." What will make you [believers] realize that even if a sign came to them they still would not believe? And We would make their hearts and their eyes turn away, just as they did not believe the first time, and leave them to flounder in their obstinacy. Even if We sent the angels down to them, and the dead spoke to them, and We gathered all things right in front of them, they still would not believe, unless God so willed, but most of them are ignorant [of this]. (6:109–11)

In addition to this is the subjective and even biased a priori sorting out of data, into important and trivial, essential and accidental, substantial and minor, real and illusory; to ensure the continuity of the credibility of already adopted supernatural and religious beliefs, sometimes even no sufficient data or no data at all is treated as supportive data! For example, for sincere believers in the existence of extraterrestrial life the lack of evidence is often interpreted as supporting evidence when linked and explained by governments' active efforts to keep the data hidden from the public.

This human tendency in religious thinking to prioritize preconception to reasoning and imitation to innovation is challenged in the Qur'an. In so many verses evidence (*burhān*) is identified as a single operative factor capable of sorting beliefs adopted out of prejudice from what can be really considered authentic and credible. In Q. 2:111 the Prophet is instructed to use this assessment method in his debates and arguments as a way to rebut wishful thinking, "This is their own wishful thinking. [Prophet], say, 'Produce your evidence (*burhān*), if you are telling the truth.'" The same concept is emphasized in, "Have they chosen to worship other gods instead of Him? Say, 'Bring your proof (*burhān*). This is the Scripture for those who are with me and the Scripture for those who went before me.' But most of them do not recognize the truth, so they pay no heed" (21:24). In Q. 23:117 the Qur'an criticizes those who worship gods other than God. But more importantly, their worship is condemned, mainly, for lacking evidence. Adding the expression "a god for which he has no evidence (*burhān*)" highlights providing evidence as the criterion one should seek for a sound religious experience. "Whoever prays to another god alongside Him—a god for which he has no evidence (*burhān*)—will face his reckoning with his Lord." Prophets themselves were provided an evidence-based experience alongside the revelation they received. While this evidence remains reason-based and far from what can be described as sensible, the fulfillment of this prerequisite is documented in so many places in the Qur'an. For example, in chapter 28 the divine encounter between Moses and God was preceded by two proofs that supported the presence of God made in "I am God, the Lord of the Worlds" as we read in,

> But when he reached it, a voice called out to him from the right-hand side of the valley, from a tree on the blessed ground: "Moses, I am God, the Lord of the Worlds. [31] Throw down your staff." When he saw his staff moving like a snake, he fled in fear and would not return. Again [he was called]: "Moses! Draw near! Do not be afraid, for you are one of those who are safe. Put your hand inside your cloak and it will come out white but unharmed—hold your arm close to your side, free from all fear. These shall be two signs (*burhān*) from your Lord to Pharaoh and his chiefs; they are truly wicked people." (28:30–32)

In chapter 2, Prophet Abraham asked for a divine evidence to put his heart at rest as the Qur'an confirms. The evidence was provided as the following verse describes, "And when Abraham said, 'My Lord, show me how You give life to the dead,' He said, 'Do you not believe, then?' 'Yes,' said Abraham, 'but just to put my heart at rest.' So God said, 'Take four birds and train them to come back to you. Then place them on separate hilltops, call them back, and they will come flying to you: know that God is all powerful and wise'" (2:260).

(7) Religious thinking is collective thinking by definition: Another difficulty stems from the fact that human religiosity in general is mass-driven and not individually adopted. Religion as a collective set of behaviors serves needs that individuals fulfil mainly when in a group. Henry Kellerman explains,

> Frequently, a blame psychology is essentially the condition of faith-based belief (whether theist or atheist) and becomes fanatical (or leading to fanaticism) as in caste systems of scapegoating or in racial discriminations, as well as in other forms of the quest to be superior—including those of political ideologies. In addition, the need for superiority can, in a practical sense, generate behavior on the basis of palpable hysteria activated by the excessive unity, chauvinistic nationalism, and cohesive togetherness (especially in the form of high cohesion), that then is enthusiastically embraced and expressed by a group.[13]

A common and easily observable tendency, one that is collective, human, and cross-religious, is to adopt a biased approach to religion, when we compare what we consider our religious reality to others' religious realities. Because in fact, what we really compare is nothing but the best in our religion to the worst in others' religions. This subconscious cognitive process ensures, in one way or another, the superiority of our previously adopted beliefs prior to any comparison. It even assures the a priori continuity of this superiority every time a comparison is made in future. On this biased assurance of superiority, Henry Kellerman (b. 1938) says,

> Generally, the need for validation of superiority, or of the need to blame, or, in an overall sense of the need to join with others in order to achieve an inner sense of security (by identifying with like-minded people), or the belief that others need to be brought to some elevated frame of thinking, is frequently found in the affiliation with a group characterized by a specific ideological identity. This focus on "my belief is the true one while yours is not" is ubiquitously seen in religious and political groups. It is certainly true that voluntary affiliation with such a group that resonates with one's needs in a congruent way, can offer exquisite peace of mind and a sense of safety. Further, reassurance of one's needs is also gained in a group affiliation where the search for mentors, icons, idols, or simply people to admire, are available.[14]

It is this easily observable and widespread human tendency of blind imitation of others, especially one's ancestors, that motivated Friedrich Nietzsche to wrongly think of it as biologically inherited. Motivated by this illusion, he concludes the following set of racist conclusions:

> There is no way to efface from a person's soul what his ancestors' best and most regularly liked to do: whether they were avid economizers, say, appendages of their desks and moneyboxes, modest and bourgeois in their desires, modest too in their virtues; or whether they lived in the habit of commanding from dawn to dusk, enjoying rough pleasures and along with them perhaps even rougher duties and responsibilities; or whether at a certain point they ultimately sacrificed their old privileges of birth and property in order to live for their beliefs (their "god"), as people of an unshakeable and sensitive conscience that blushes at every compromise. It is simply impossible that a person would not have his parents' and forefathers' qualities and preferences in his body—whatever appearances may say to the contrary. This is a problem of race. If we know something about the parents, then we are allowed a stab at the child: a certain repellent intemperance, a certain narrow envy, a clumsy self-righteousness (these three together have ever made up the true rabble type)—these things will be passed on to the child as surely as corrupted blood; and all that the best upbringing or education can achieve is to deceive others about such an inheritance.[15]

The Qur'an affirms individualism as a core component of the human experience of religion in so many places. For example, the Qur'an criticizes religiosity that is merely inherited, lock, stock, and barrel, adopted without active effort to use reason, sift, and question, "Most of them do not use reason: [104] when it is said to them, 'Come to what God has sent down, and to the Messenger,' they say, 'What we inherited from our forefathers is good enough for us,' even though their forefathers knew nothing and were not guided" (5:103–104). In one scene from the hereafter the Qur'an describes how those who have been followed disown their own followers, "When those who have been followed disown their followers, when they all see the suffering, when all bonds between them are severed, [167] the followers will say, 'If only we had one last chance, we would disown them as they now disown us'" (2:166–67). More interesting though, the blind-follower attitude is not excused in the Qur'an even in cases where following is not motivated by full consent but by mere fear, and unless it is totally impossible to escape: "When the angels take the souls of those who have wronged themselves, they ask them, 'What circumstances were you in?' They reply, 'We were oppressed in this land,' and the angels say, 'But was God's earth not spacious enough for you to migrate to some other place?' These people will have Hell as their refuge, an evil destination, but not so the truly helpless men, women, and children who have no means in their power nor any way to leave—God may well pardon these, for He is most pardoning and most forgiving" (4:97–100).

(8) Religious thinking is wishful thinking by definition: Many times, we subconsciously choose our beliefs, including religious beliefs, for merely pragmatic reasons. We subconsciously dismiss and turn away from beliefs that can cause us a high price for adopting. Changing religion, conversion, apostasy, denying adopted rituals, or even rethinking religion, all come with a price that the majority of people are not ready to pay. The Qur'an openly criticized those who consciously choose not to choose God, not out of innocent ignorance, but out of prioritizing—almost everything and everyone—to God as we read in, "Say [Prophet], 'If your fathers, sons, brothers, wives, tribes, the wealth you have acquired, the trade which you fear will decline, and the dwellings you love are dearer to you than God and His Messenger and the struggle in His cause, then wait until God brings about His punishment.' God does not guide those who break away" (Q. 9:24). However, the real threat to the same concept of religiosity doesn't come from those clear cases in which people rationally choose to prioritize benefit, others opinions, or even family to one's more sincere religious stance; but from knotty cases where people think of themselves as devout believers without realizing that what lies under their religious adherence is nothing but a subconscious avoidance of undesired consequences. Some of these undesired consequences can include, but are not limited to, losing supporting social networks, failing family members, marital conflicts, failing to live up to others' expectations, individually facing others' mockery or rejection, losing a job or a promotion, and so forth. To be clear, adopting or rejecting a religious belief does not commonly go through a conscious analysis of benefits and consequences but is merely subconsciously motivated by the feeling(s) that a belief or a certain set of beliefs can trigger. This is what Richard Dawkins (b. 1941) refers to by saying, "It is amazing how many people seemingly cannot tell the difference between 'X is true' and 'It is desirable that people should believe that X is true.' Or maybe they don't really fall for this logical error, but simply rate truth as unimportant compared with human feelings."[16]

On the top of the list of the subconscious, more pragmatic, values comes our human tendency to resist change. This is what explains why we prioritize criticizing others' beliefs and highlighting their shortcomings to criticizing our own. Finding what is wrong in others' realities is easier because it doesn't require any change. Other than feelings of pity, discontent, or even anger, disagreeing with others' beliefs—even if off the wall—does not invoke feelings of shame, guilt, regret, and fallibility, which self-criticizing can ignite. But more importantly, criticizing others does not require any change on our part. We often run with beliefs that do not require change. This is what explains the fierce battles reformers, pioneers, and seekers of change in every religion have to fight. Many times, the resistance of change from the inside is stronger and even more violent than the resistance from outsiders. Burning books, accusations of blasphemy, describing new ways of thinking as heretical innovations, physical torture, and even execution all constitute the same sort of practices hostile to change that have been historically repeated in almost all religions. What can be even more challenging—psychologically speaking—than adopting new beliefs is the departure from those that are collectively adopted. Criticizing blind imitation of others is a recurring theme in the Qur'an as we read in, "when it is said to them, 'Come to what God has sent down, and to the Messenger,' they say, 'What we inherited from our forefathers is good enough for us,' even though their forefathers knew nothing and were not guided" (4:104).

(9) Religious thinking is unverifiable by definition: What do *kufr* (disbelief) and *īmān* (faith) stand for from a pure Qur'anic perspective? How can one assess both? How can we measure one's religious commitment or faithfulness? It is important to note that the Qur'an precisely condemns only those who *intentionally* deny the religious truth after *it was made clear to them*. This subtle pinpointing addresses the many difficulties surrounding the way we adopt religious beliefs and narrows down the concept of disbelief to a very specific category, namely, those who denounce religious reality *after* having recognized it as a reality. More importantly, it motivates us to rethink God's justice. According to the Qur'anic criterion, unless the agent becomes cognitively aware of religious reality *as a reality* and then decides to deny it for reasons other than genuine ignorance, he or she cannot be considered blameworthy. In other words—ironically enough—no one in the Qur'an becomes a disbeliever before becoming a believer first. Judging one's faith goes beyond the superficial human abilities and requires a divine ability that exceeds the blasphemy accusations people usually satisfy by bombarding each other with. This recognition is supported variably in the Qur'an. First, it is supported by the textual evidence of cognitive awareness and intentionality as a condition for holding the agent responsible and accountable in case he or she decides to reject religious reality. Let us consider the following verse, "There are some of them who twist the Scripture with their tongues to make you [people] think that what they say is part of the Scripture when it is not; they say it is from God when it is not; they attribute lies to God and they know it" (3:78). In this verse, adding the expression "and they know it" to attributing lies to God would have been redundant if "telling lies about God" is all what the verse is really addressing. It is the intentional and advertent denial of the divine message after recognizing it as authentic and divine that the text precisely attacks here. In other words, it is the deliberate falsification of the sacred text that is condemned by the verse and not the mere confusion in terms of interpreting, narrating, or conveying the text, which may be accidental or arbitrary. Likewise, concealing religious reality only after recognizing it as a reality is what the Qur'an asserts as accountable in the following verse,

"People of the Book, why do you mix truth with falsehood? Why do you hide the truth when you recognize it?" (3:71). Similar to the previous analysis, adding the expression "when you recognize it" to hiding the truth would have been redundant if hiding the truth is all what matters from a Qur'anic perspective. As the Qur'an confirms, what matters is hiding the truth only after it is fully comprehended as true. Even the rejection of divine signs and miracles is only accountable after the full realization of them as divine signs takes place, as we read in, "But when Our enlightening signs came to them, they said, 'This is clearly [just] sorcery! They denied them, in their wickedness and their pride, even though their souls acknowledged them as true" (27:13–14). Denial, then, as motivated by pride and wickedness is what the Qur'anic verses address and not denial as motivated by mere ignorance. Second, in a meaningful way the Qur'an refers to the following chronological order as we read in, "Why would God guide people who deny the truth, after they have believed and acknowledged that the Messenger is true, and after they have been shown clear proof? God does not guide evil-doers" (Q. 10: 86). True infidelity then should be essentially preceded by a recognition of the soundness and the authenticity of what one might take an informative decision to deny and reject. Third, the repeated affirmations in the Qur'an of the need to make religion as clear as possible as the main religious duty of everyone, including prophets, confirms comprehending religious truth as true and authentic as a condition for accountability. "We have sent down the message to you too [Prophet], so that you can explain to people what was sent for them, so that they may reflect" (16:43). Sending a messenger is even considered as a Qur'anic abiding condition for human accountability as we read in, "Whoever accepts guidance does so for his own good; whoever strays does so at his own peril. No soul will bear another's burden, nor do We punish until We have sent a messenger" (Q. 17:15). Fourth, the Qur'an confirms religious accountability as an exclusive divine right. No prophet or religious authority according to the Qur'an is given the right to question, assess, or even evaluate the faithfulness of anyone or to take them accountable based on their beliefs, "He knows best who is mindful of Him" (53:32). Even Prophet Muhammad is not given that right as we read in many places like, "So [Prophet] remind them; your only task is to remind, [22] you are not there to control them" (88:21). Fifth, in a meaningful way the Qur'an uses the same word *kuffār* (sing. *kāfir*; disbeliever) in Q. 75:20 in a nonnegative way[17] to refer to farmers who cover seeds in the ground and then to disbelievers in the rest of the Qur'an. "Bear in mind that the present life is just a game, a diversion, an attraction, a cause of boasting among you, of rivalry in wealth and children. It is like plants that spring up after the rain; their growth at first delights the sowers (*kuffār*), but then you see them wither away, turn yellow, and become stubble." As Ibn Qutayba explains, the Arabic root *k-f-r* in Q. 53:32 applies to anything that stands for covering.[18] The analogy is clear between farmers who cover seeds in the ground and disbelievers identified here as those who cover the truth after their full recognition of it.

(10) Religious thinking is fallible by definition: The epistemic gap between our human understanding and the transcendental nature of the religious text lies at the heart of what religion as a test and as an epistemic hardship means. Criticizing others' subjective and even prejudice reading of the Qur'anic text doesn't render our reading more complete or less imperfect. Rather, it aims at highlighting our humanity and acknowledges one basic shortcoming that we all share as humans: fallibility. Reading a divine text doesn't make us divine and the customary manner we use, in initiating reading the Qurʾanic text, by saying "this is what God said" is best understood as a metaphorical reference to what we believe to have been said by God, as Ziauddin Sardar (b. 1951) aptly elaborates:

> A divine text does not yield a divine meaning: the meaning attributed to it can only be the product of human understanding. A timeless book has meaning only in time. It can only speak to us in our own time and circumstances. Our understanding of "the Final Word of God" cannot be final. It can only be transitory and limited by our own abilities and understanding. It gives us intimations of the divine, the mind of God, but by definition, however perfectible we may think humankind is, we are not and cannot be the mind of God. Absolute understanding, absolute certainty, infallible knowledge—these are not attributes of humanity; our lot is wrestling with our all too evident limitations. Therefore, the "Word of God" is not beyond question: only through questioning the text can we tease out possible answers to our moral dilemmas. This is precisely why one of the most insistent commands in the Qurʾān is to think and reflect.[19]

The gap between the religious text and our understandings of it is not a mere theoretical observation but a proven historical fact as well. More importantly, the variety and even the contradicting nature of interpretations are not the mere result of conflicts in understanding, but are oftentimes motivated by pragmatic attempts to use and even to manipulate authority by claiming an (or *the*) exclusive right to the religious text. Naṣr Ḥāmid Abū Zayd (1943–2010) explains the way "the authority of the text"[20] was first used in early Islamic political, social, and ideological conflicts by the Umayyads, who gave it a semiotic and ideological meaning by asking their soldiers to fix copies of the Qur'an on their swords in the Battle of Ṣiffīn.[21] In other words, many times the variety of the human understanding of the same religious text is not the result of mere theoretical schisms per se but a deliberate attempt to reshape the text for pure pragmatic reasons by "a group that adopts the text and turns it to an authority."[22] Even ideologies, as Abū Zayd argues, "by adopting the textual language become religious."[23]

Realizing and theologically internalizing the previously discussed difficulties raise key questions: How can we believe in God without knowing Him or His attributes? How can religious thinking still live up to credibility and reliability? More importantly, how does one set apart "rational faith" from "blind faith"? The essence of the religious experience is to use revelation-based clues as guidance for rationalizing faith. Faith or religious belief as based on (empirical) knowledge can hardly be called faith. The Qur'an asserts as much in many places. Religion as a test and an epistemic hardship lies at the core of human religiosity. Nullifying this aspect, as in the case of revealing final prophecies, for example, means nothing—as the Qur'an asserts—but the end of our religious experience as God's successors on earth. Therefore, this does not happen—as the Qur'an explains—before the end and the destruction of the world, as we know it takes place, "We have brought people a Scripture—We have explained it on the basis of true knowledge—as guidance and mercy for those who believe. What are they waiting for but the fulfilment of its [final prophecy]? One the Day it is fulfilled, those who had ignored it will say, 'Our Lord's messenger spoke the truth'" (7:52–53). As this verse asserts, belief as based on empirical knowledge—which takes place once all and every epistemic hardship is removed—does not constitute sound belief in the first place. Sound religious belief is based on revelation, which should predate and not follow experience-based empirical belief. Belief, as the Qur'an asserts, loses all merit once all and every associated epistemic hardship is over, "Are they waiting for the very angels to come to them, or your Lord Himself, or some of His signs? But on the Day some of your Lord's signs come, no soul will profit from faith if it had none before, or has already earned some good through its faith" (6:158). Religion as a divine test is a prerequisite for the soundness of our religious experience as humans. Therefore, the request to remove the test by way of sending confirming signs, working miracles—even temporarily—or worse by way of asking to see God Himself is portrayed in the Qur'an as an unjustifiable demand. An unjust request made to Moses to see God ended by a severe punishment as we read, "Remember when you said, 'Moses, we will not believe you until we see God face to face.' At that, thunderbolts struck you as you looked on" (2:55). The fulfilment of similar requests temporarily interrupts the divine plan for humans on earth, that is, it deactivates the religion as an epistemic hardship.

Therefore, when a request of this type is answered it is usually followed by binding consequences as we read in many places in the Qur'an. One striking example is a request of sending down a divine sign that was addressed to Jesus by his disciples. This request ended with a binding obligation as a requirement for its fulfilment as we read:

> When the disciples said, "Jesus, son of Mary, can your Lord send down a feast to us from heaven?" He said, "Beware of God if you are true believers." They said, "We wish to eat from it; to have our hearts reassured; to know that you have told us the truth; and to be witnesses of it." Jesus, son of Mary, said, "Lord, send down to us a feat from heaven so that we can have a festival—the first and last of us—and a sign from you. Provide for us: You are the best provider." God said, "I will send it down to you, but anyone who disbelieves after this will be punished with a punishment that I will not inflict on anyone else in the world." (5:112–15)

In the Qur'anic story of Saleh—like in others—the story ends with a divine punishment. The punishment does not come as many might wrongly think for choosing not to believe in God. Rather, the divine punishment comes as a result of rejecting God after asking to remove the epistemic hardship—which essentially accompanies religion as a human test—by way of demonstrating a divine sign. As many Qur'anic verses attest, the she-camel of God was sent to Saleh's people upon their request as a miracle. "A clear sign has come to you now from your Lord: this is God's she-camel—a sign for you—so let her graze in God's land and do not harm her in any way, or you will be struck by a painful torment" (7:73). Removing the epistemic hardship by way of sending the she-camel is the reason Saleh's people were punished afterward when they denied what they have already requested, "They said, 'You are bewitched! You are nothing but a man like us. Show us a sign, if you are telling the truth. He said, 'Here is a camel. She should have her turn to drink and so should you, each on a specific day, so do not harm her, or the torment of a terrible day will befall you'" (26:153–56). It is their overt rejection of God after and not before their "epistemic hardship" was removed which caused them torment after they challenged God and "hamstrung her" (26:157). In the story of Noah, who is mostly famous for the Flood, the final episode does not come without the assertion of miracles and signs that were rejected by his people as the cause of the Flood, as we read in, "and We helped him against the people who rejected Our signs—they were evil people, so We drowned them all" (21:77).

God, as the Qur'an confirms in these and other stories, does not simply make people atone for their denial or ungrateful religious attitude in the worldly life and before the Day of Judgment. All cases of worldly assigned divine punishment have one thing in common: a denial after a request of nullifying religion, as a test, when an epistemic hardship is fulfilled. Removing epistemic hardship, even temporarily, announces the end of our assigned worldly test and leaves no excuse for rejecters, after faith turns from a revelation-based cognitive belief to an experience-based empirical belief. Interpreting God's torment in Qur'anic stories as caused by humanity's recalcitrance leaves behind the fact that, other than in some specific stories that all share removing episteme hardship as a common denominator, the Qur'an does not commend worldly consequences for rejecting faith, "If anyone desires [only] the fleeting life, We speed up whatever We will in it, for whoever We wish; in the end We have prepared Hell for him in which to burn, disgraced and rejected. But if anyone desires the life to come and strives towards it as he should, as a true believer, his striving will be thanked. To both the latter and the former, We give some of your Lord's bounty. [Prophet], your Lord's bounty is not restricted" (17:18–20).

Why should revelation-based belief proceed empirical-based belief as an essential condition for the soundness of our religious experience? I argue in chapter 3 for free will as an irreplaceable condition that not only made humans qualify to become God's successors on earth, but also confirms their earthly divinity. I also explain this condition as essential to the degree that it cannot be canceled as long as there are people making choices, be they good or bad. Now, turning belief into an experience-based empirical experience means the cancellation of free will by way of providing what is too profound, too compelling, and even too unequivocal for humans to neglect or refuse. To explain, what choice is left for humans in terms of accepting or rejecting God's divinity once tangible cosmological and supernatural evidence is provided? This option deactivates free will by turning faith and religion in general from a voluntary experience into a compulsory experience. While the first experience is what is initially intended for God's chosen successors on earth, the second experience is the experience of all other beings. As we read in the Qur'an, angels have an empirical-based experience (and belief) of God. Angels, though, were not chosen for succeeding God on earth in the first place. The Qur'an, for example, explains the angels' firsthand experience of God's throne as we read, "Those [angels] who carry the Throne and those who surround it celebrate the praise of their Lord and have faith in Him" (40:7). As I argue in this book, angels can, but do not, choose evil. This firsthand experience of God might be one explaining reason. But does it nullify their free will? The answer is no, for the simple reason angels are not assigned as divine successors on earth the way humans are. Therefore, concealing such an experience is not as essential for them as it is for humans. Angels are not assigned religion as a test nor as an epistemic hardship. Revealing disclosed religious reality can deactivate human free will and end the merit of their earthly assignment on earth but does not deactivate angels' free will, because angels, unlike humans, do not have an earthly assignment as successors. Perhaps free will as provided to angels is similar to free will that will be granted to humans after the end of their assignment on earth. Perhaps in the afterworld, humans, like angels, will experience belief in God that is empirical. This type of belief will turn them into beings that—like angels—can, but do not, choose evil. The afterworld's being based on experience and belief of God that is empirical is confirmed many times in the Qur'an. Believers in the hereafter will be "looking towards their Lord" (75:23).[24] Also, as the Qur'an confirms, believers will be communicating with angels, "This is the way God rewards the righteous, those whose lives the angels take in a state of goodness. They will say to them, 'Peace be upon you. Enter the Garden as a reward for what you have done'" (16:32).

Interestingly enough, empirical belief in God in this world is experienced by animals and nonrational beings, in addition to angels. This type of knowledge is purposefully and intentionally hidden only from humans, who are exclusively assigned the honor of succeeding God on earth. Such experience is confirmed many times in the Qur'an, which describes the sun, the moon, stars mountains, trees, animals, and plants as beings that prostrate (*yasjudu*) to God as in Q. 55:6, and as we read in, "Do you not realize [Prophet] that everything in the heavens and earth submits (*yasjudu*) to God: the sun, the moon, the stars, the mountains, the trees, and the animals?" (22:18). In chapter 17 we read, "The seven heavens and the earth and everyone in them glorify Him. There is not a single thing that does not celebrate His praise, though you do not understand their praise" (17:44). Also, we read, "We made the mountains and birds celebrate Our praises with David" (21:79). Another example still can be found in the story of Queen Sheba where the hoopoe says to Solomon,

> I have learned something you did not know: I come to you from Sheba with firm news. I found a woman ruling over the people, who has been given a share of everything—she has a magnificent throne—[but] I found that she and her people worshiped the sun instead of God. Satan has made their deeds seem alluring to them, and diverted them from the right path: they cannot find the right path. Should they not worship God, who brings forth what is hidden in the heavens and earth and knows both what you people conceal and what you declare? He is God, there is no god but Him, the Lord of the mighty throne. (27:22–25)

Mere observation-based knowledge or empirical knowledge doesn't provide much help, then, when applied to religious knowledge. The previously discussed obstacles and challenges makes religious knowledge a human test par excellence. The Qur'an asserts reflection when guided by revelation as a way that humans can seek instead. Therefore, reminding humans of their divinely provided cognitive capacities comes as a recurring theme in the Qur'an. In Q. 7:176, like in many other places in the Qur'an, the text uses the form *tafāʿala* to assert "the continuity" of the verb,[25] or the continuity of reflection as a human responsibility, "Tell them the story so that they may reflect." As the Qur'an confirms, signs in the heavens and earth can speak only to those who use their reason, "There are signs in the heavens and the earth for those who believe [4] in the creation of you, in the creatures God scattered on earth, there are signs for people of sure faith, [5] in the alteration of night and day, in the rain God provides, sending it down from the sky and reviving the dead earth with it, and His shifting of the winds there are signs for those who use their reason" (45:3–5). Those who do not use their reason are condemned in the Qur'an for behaving like animals, having neglected their human faculty of reasoning, as we read in, "Do you think that most of them hear or understand? They are just like cattle—no, they are further from the path" (25:44). Even revelation, as the Qur'an asserts, is sent down such that "those with understanding take heed" as we read in, "This is a blessed Scripture, which We have sent down to you [Muhammad], so that people may think about its messages and those with understanding take heed" (38:29).

In this chapter, I presented challenges associated with religion, which, I argue, is an ultimate test for humans as God's gods on earth. Many challenges associated with religious beliefs are better understood as part of the meaning of human religiosity, though. These challenges are not mentioned in an effort to undermine human religiosity; to the contrary, they are highlighted in an effort to unearth the seriousness of the human mission as God's gods on earth. From a Qur'anic perspective, navigating a righteous religious path while surrounded by all these challenges is a mission available only for the elite. Because "only those who are steadfast in patience, only those who are blessed with great righteousness, will attain to such goodness" (41:35). Acknowledging the multilevel complexities involved in adopting or departing from any religious belief provides a better approach to understanding religion. Unfortunately, the strategy adopted by some traditional apologetics, who try to face these challenges by denying their existence, belittling their seriousness, or prioritizing blind imitation and cultic adherence instead, keeps deviating from the Qur'anic message in a world that keeps moving away from religion. On the other end of the spectrum, citing some or all of these difficulties as antireligious arguments—a process that has been snowballing since the Enlightenment's first announcement of its divorce from religion—fails to appreciate what religion stands for in the first place. In chapter 3, I move from discussing the idea of religion as a test and an epistemic hardship that defines humans' divine status and merit, to using the concept of testing as a key to solving the problem of evil.

## NOTES

1. Mary Pat Fisher, *Living Religions* (Boston, MA: Prentice Hall, 2011), 15.
2. Riḍā, *Tafsīr al-manār*, 9:189.

3. Ibn Ḥazm al-Andalusī, *al-Fiṣal fī l-milal wa-l-ahwā' wa-l-niḥal* (Cairo: Maktabat al-Salām al-ʿIlmiyya, 1923), 3:2.

4. Muḥammad b. Aḥmad al-Saffārīnī, *al-Buḥūr al-zākhira fī ʿulum al-ākhira* (Riyadh: Dār al-ʿĀṣima, 2008), 1213.

5. I do not discuss the well-known debate in *kalām* concerning the afterlife experience of God, confining myself instead, here, to the worldly experience of God.

6. ʿAbd al-Laṭīf al-Kharbūtī, *Tanqīḥ al-kalām fī ʿaqā'id ahl al-Islām* (Istanbul: Najm Istiqbāl Maṭbaʿasī, 1912), 229.

7. Like in "Pavlovian conditioning."

8. Sven Schottmann and Joseph Camilleri, "Culture, Religion and the Southeast Asian State," in *Culture, Religion and Conflict in Muslim Southeast Asia: Negotiating Tense Pluralisms*, ed. Joseph Camilleri and Sven Schottmann (London: Routledge, 2012), 3.

9. Taqī al-Dīn Aḥmad b. ʿAbd al-Ḥalīm Ibn Taymiyya, *al-Risāla al-madaniyya fī taḥqīq al-majāz wa-l-ḥaqīqa fī ṣifāt Allāh Taʿāla* (Riyadh: al-Sunna al-Muḥammadiyya, 2000), 40. The historical debate regarding the divine attributes is irrelevant to my discussion, which is limited to the epistemic difficulty involved in understanding these attributes and how the debate is extended to the ontological status of these attributes.

10. Jalāl al-Dīn Rūmī, *Signs of the Unseen: The Discourses of Jalaluddin Rumi*, trans. W. M. Thackston, Jr. (Boston, MA, and London: Shambhala, 1999), 183.

11. Jābir b. Idrīs b. ʿAlī Amīr, *Maqālat al-tashbīh wa-mawqif ahl al-sunna minhā* (Cairo: Dār Aḍwā' al-Salaf, 2002), 1:145.

12. Bryan Caplan, *The Myth of the Rational Voter* (Princeton, NJ: Princeton University Press, 2007), 2.

13. Henry Kellerman, *The Discovery of God* (New York: Springer, 2013), 50.

14. Ibid.

15. Friedrich Nietzsche, *Beyond Good and Evil: Prelude to a Philosophy of the Future*, trans. Marion Faber (New York: Oxford University Press, 1998), 161.

16. Richard Dawkins, *The God Delusion* (New York: Houghton Mifflin Company, 2006), 353.

17. Riḍā, *Tafsīr al-manār*, 3:20.

18. ʿAbd Allāh b. Muslim Ibn Qutayba, *Ta'wīl mushkil al-Qur'ān* (Cairo: al-Ḥalabī, 1900), 54.

19. Ziauddin Sardar, *Reading the Qur'an: The Contemporary Relevance of the Sacred Text of Islam* (Oxford and New York: Oxford University Press, 2011), 10.

20. Naṣr Ḥāmid Abū Zayd, *al-Naṣṣ al-sulṭa al-ḥaqīqa* (Beirut: al-Markaz al-Thaqāfī al-ʿArabī, 1995), 113.

21. Alexander Mikaberidze, *Conflict and Conquest in the Islamic World* (Santa Barbara, CA: ABC-CLIO, 2011), 1:836.

22. Naṣr Ḥāmid Abū Zayd, *al-Tafkīr fī zaman al-takfīr* (Cairo: Maktaba Madbūlī,1995), 138.

23. Abū Zayd, *al-Naṣṣ al-sulṭa al-ḥaqīqa*, 115.

24. The long theological debate concerning the possibility of seeing God in the hereafter, involving the Muʿtazilites, Jahmites, Khawārij, Ashʿarites, and others, goes beyond what I am more interested in discussing here. In addition, negating the

possibility of such an experience in the afterlife contradicts the mainstream Sunni consensus and the overt and literal Qur'anic confirmation.

25. Badr al-Dīn al-ʿAynī, *ʿUmdat al-qāriʾ: Sharḥ Ṣaḥīḥ al-Bukhārī* (Beirut: Dār al-Kutub al-ʿIlmiyya, 2001), 7:78.

## *Chapter 3*

# Rethinking the Divine Status of Humans

## *A Key to Solving the Problem of Evil*

A recurring theological question that ignited, and is still igniting, all types of debates is the question: How can a just God allow evil? In *Dialogues concerning Natural Religion* David Hume (1711–1776) famously asks the question, "Is he willing to prevent evil, but not able? Then is he impotent. Is he able, but not willing? Then is he malevolent. Is he both able and willing? Whence then is evil?"[1] The problematic aspect of allowing evil while having the ability to stop it causes many to deny either the existence of God, the existence of a just God, or even the existence of a God powerful enough to stop evil. This chapter uses the divine status of humans as a key to address these questions.

### THE PROBLEM OF "HUMAN EVIL"

I argued previously that God created Adam as a successive authority and as a divine deputy on earth. In addition, I argued that Adam and his offspring were given a divine challenge. By passing the test of religion as an "epistemic hardship" humans can prove their merit and reclaim their divine status and right to paradise. However, morally speaking, making merit-worthy choices requires free will as a necessary condition. Therefore, humans are given this right unconditionally and unrestrictedly. According to the divine contract between God and Adam, consequences of exercising the right of choice do not constitute a reason good enough to nullify the contract. Because the contract was essentially established on the bases of granting Adam a divine status, ending Adam's divine status by intervening in the discourse of exercising his rights as the divine on earth is nothing but a violation of the divine contract. In this section, I argue for the existence of "human evil," which stands for unwanted and undesired outcomes of humans' exercising their unconditional right to free will. Human evil exists as an option, temporarily allowed yet not desired by God. More importantly, this affirmation of the existence of human evil does not contradict the existence of a just God. My Qur'anic-based argument for human evil, usually referred to as "moral evil," as a divinely allowed, but not divinely desired, option is supported by the following observations.

(1) According to the Qur'anic divine contract between God, on the one hand, Adam and his offspring, on the other, Adam was sent down as a trusted "successor on earth" (2:30). This contract was finalized in the Qur'an the following way, "[Prophet], when your Lord took out the offspring from the loins of the Children of Adam and made them bear witness about themselves, He said, 'Am I not your Lord?' and they replied, 'Yes, we bear witness.' So you cannot say on the Day of Resurrection, 'We were not aware of this'" (7:172). By definition, a successor is assigned on behalf of the original authority to exercise all powers given by the former. An intervention to stop evil consequences of any human choice, good or bad, is a nullification of the contract.

(2) According to the Qur'anic contract, the timed divine assignment of humans as God's gods on earth ends only at the Day of Judgment. While I stress in the first point human free will as the basic condition in the contract, I am highlighting here the contract as a temporary one. Any intervention to stop human evil or to correct human conduct or even to reward or punish humans for their behavior before the Day of Judgment is a violation of the timed contract. In the Qur'an the Day of Judgment is described as the day when authority returns to God in a clear confirmation of the absence of divine authority before then, as we read, "On the Day when the sky and its clouds are split apart and the angels sent down in streams, on that Day, true authority belongs to the Lord of Mercy" (25:25–26). In so many places in the Qur'an the text strictly confirms that no divine intervention will be allowed before the Day of Judgment, as in, "On the Day of Resurrection, God will judge between you regarding your differences" (22:69) and, "God will judge between them on the Day of Resurrection concerning their differences" (2:113). In other words, humans continue to be given the authority to act as divine regardless of the merit of their deeds until the Day of Judgment. In addition, any divine intervention to stop evil before the Day of Judgment turns the same concept into a superfluous idea. If justice were to be totally established in the worldly life, what would be left for the Day of Judgment? Alternatively, if justice were to be partially and selectively established in the worldly life, what would be the criteria for such a selective approach? Would such a discriminatory approach in dealing with some evils and leaving others behind be just in the first place?

(3) The Qur'anic text clearly and literally addresses the problem of the existence of a human evil that is postponed, to be properly dealt with only once the divine contract is over. In other words, the Qur'an doesn't seem to be ignoring but acknowledging the existence of a problem that will be dealt with following the expiration of the divine contract. This literal acknowledgment is found, for example, in, "Do not think [Prophet] that God is unaware of what the disbelievers do: He only gives them respect until a Day when their eyes will stare in terror" (14:42). The Qur'an doesn't deny the existence of evil (*sharr*), unlike those who try to deal with the problem of evil by ignoring its reality. To the contrary, evil is confirmed in many places in the Qur'an, as in, "If God were to hasten on for people the harm (*sharr*) [they have earned] as they wish to hasten on the good, their time would already be up" (10:11). Also in the Qur'an, we read about Joseph ascribing evil to his brothers as he says to himself, "[His brothers] said, 'If he is a thief then his brother was a thief before him,' but Joseph kept his secrets and did not reveal anything to them. He said, 'You are in a far worse (*sharr*) situation. God knows best the truth of what you claim'" (12:77). Further, we read about the existence of evil in, "Whenever We are gracious to man, he goes away haughtily, but, as soon as harm (*sharr*) touches him, he turns to prolonged prayer" (41:51).

Rethinking the Qur'anic text reveals a consideration of evil as a human, and not a divine, responsibility. "Why did you say, when a calamity befell you, even after you had inflicted twice as much damage [on your enemy], 'How did this happen?' [Prophet], say, 'You brought it upon yourselves.' God has power over everything" (3:165). Interestingly enough, in the Qur'an all unwanted outcomes can be categorized as the result of humanity's propensity for corruption, including that of the natural world, usually referred to as "natural evil." "Corruption has flourished on land and sea as a result of people's actions and He will make them taste the consequences of some of their own actions so that they may turn back" (30:41).

What the Qur'an denies, though, is "divine evil" as we read, "God does not wrong people at all—it is they who wrong themselves" (10:44). In the story of creation, we see the Devil adopting a God-blaming attitude by saying, "'Because You have put me in the wrong, I will lie in wait for them all on Your straight path'" (7:16). Instead of adopting such an attitude, the Qur'an asks humans to consider God not as the source of evil but as the refuge that can be sought for all kinds of protection from evil, either as caused by other humans or as caused by Satan, "Say [Prophet], 'I seek refuge with the Lord of daybreak against the harm (*sharr*) of what He has created, the harm (*sharr*) of the night when darkness gathers, the harm (*sharr*) of witches when they blow on knots, the harm (*sharr*) of the envier when he envies'" (113:1–5). In the famous story of Job, the prophet practically adopts this approach as he blamed Satan for his calamities and sought help from no one but God. Not only were his prayers answered, as the Qur'an confirms, in addition, he was acknowledged and praised as "an excellent servant!" (38:44): "Bring to mind Our servant Job who cried to his Lord, 'Satan has afflicted me with weariness and suffering.' 'Stamp your foot! Here is cool water for you to wash and drink,' and We restored his family to him, with many more like them: a sign of Our mercy and a lesson to all who understand" (38:41–43).

The Qur'anic acknowledgment of human evil as an outcome of bad human choices implements punishment in the hereafter as necessary for bringing criminals to ultimate justice. Unlike a popular line of argument that tries to advocate for religion by portraying God as a merciful deity who rewards but never punishes, praises but never reproaches, loves but never hates, the Qur'anic image of God draws our attention to a deity who does not turn his back to the wronged but acknowledges fair punishment as a way to address "human evil," which—otherwise—would be left inadequately addressed. Chapter 85 in the Qur'an describes the punishment assigned for a group who tortured believers. This chapter addresses the same concern that many might raise concerning a God who doesn't immediately react to human suffering. Interestingly enough, the chapter fully and vividly describes the horrible crimes committed against a group of believers; however, instead of implementing an immediate worldly plan to stop the mentioned crimes, the chapter insists on documenting all what happened to insure the remorseful after-worldly fate those aggressors will be facing, "perish the makers of the trench, of the fuel-stoked fire! They sat down and witnessed what they were doing to the believers. Their only grievance against them was their faith in God, the Mighty, the Praiseworthy, to whom all control over the heavens and earth belongs: God is witness over all things. For those who persecute believing men and women, and do not repent afterwards, there will be the torment of Hell and burning" (85:4–10).

(4) A deity who intervenes to stop human evil every time a person chooses to bring about harm is more evil than a deity who leaves human-caused harm and evil to take place. Because, while the latter respects the full authority already given to humans on earth, even when they abuse that authority, the former is more concerned with correcting the act even if this results in the destruction of the—already granted—divine status of humans. This divine agency of humanity places humans as God's gods on earth. God doesn't act as a superior God to His deputies as long as the divine assignment on earth is still ongoing. Divine intervention includes, by definition, a sense of a divine guardianship that can end all human divine agency if humans are to be placed as God's inferior gods. The fact that God made Adam divine by breathing His own spirit into him should be reevaluated when we think of humans' worldly divine agency as one that can be violated, devalued, or arbitrarily deactivated,

"When I have fashioned him and breathed My spirit into him, bow down before him" (15:29).

(5) As the Qur'an asserts, divine guidance was sent down to humans via books, prophets, and messengers. This divine guidance is strictly conditioned by free will and is limited to what humans freely choose to do. The repeated Qur'anic messages of compulsion as foreign to what religion stands for match the full acknowledgment of divine human agency, which can't be annulled even by religious authorities. This is clear in, "There is no compulsion in religion" (2:256). Granting human beings free will without allowing them to make their own choices –including wrong choices—is a logical contradiction and a violation of the same meaning of granting free will. As Richard Swinburne (b. 1934) states, "It would seem logically impossible for God to give agents this freedom (to make it up to them how they will choose) without the probability of them making some wrong choices. The more agents who have this freedom, the more such choices they have, and the greater the temptation to wrongdoing, the more wrong choices there will probably be."[2]

(6) There is a difference between God as a deity who desires human evil and God as a deity who merely allows and temporarily tolerates it, due to respecting divine human agency. God does not orchestrate or facilitate human evil; to the contrary, "God wishes for us to repent and atone for our sins so we can enter paradise after death."[3] In the Qur'an we read, "Alas for human beings! Whenever a messenger comes to them they ridicule him" (36:30); "God creates evil not pleased by it [. . .] but for reasons He knows."[4] Evil as an unsatisfactory and undesired human choice is explained in the Qur'an: "If you are ungrateful, remember God has no need of you, yet He is not pleased by ingratitude in His servants; if you are grateful, He is pleased [to see] it in you" (39:7).

(7) God doesn't desire human evil by choosing to create beings that can choose evil. Because the opposite will be one of two options: either choosing to create beings that cannot choose evil or choosing to create beings that can but do not choose evil. As I explain, both options are problematic in our case. First, choosing to create beings that cannot choose evil means the cancellation of free will and human autonomy. This option means no more than downgrading humans from divine to robotic and from creative to merely animate. Peter Green (1871–1961) states:

> As the essence of virtue lies in free choice, the idea of any man forced to be good is a contradiction in terms. From the least matter to the greatest it is true that a man cannot be made to choose. He may be forced to accept one of two alternatives, but such acceptance, if the forced applied is really such as he could not resist, involves no moral element. If the alternative accepted is the right one, he is nevertheless deserving of no praise and in no sense virtuous. If the

> alternative is the wrong one, he is nevertheless not blame-worthy and there is no element of vice.[5]

Reconciling the concept of human suffering with divinely granted human freedom does not only help reconnect humans with their divine status but can help cope with suffering as well. David Birnbaum (b. 1950) elaborates on this:

> The aggrieved may find some comfort in the concept that this pain is, rather, part of the high price humanity pays for its freedom, and for the possibility of ultimately realizing its full potential; that the individual's tragedy was unlikely to have been punishment, and at the same time did not occur for naught; that while the particular tragedy was not part of a specific Divine plan, the allowance of tragedy in general is a cosmic necessity, and on that level may be considered part of an ultimate schema. For man must operate at an increasingly higher level of freedom if he is to have bona fide potential for a higher good—in his quest towards ultimate potentiality.[6]

Muslim theologians have famously debated the free-will question for centuries. The Qadariyya, who predated the Muʿtazilites, reject predestination. For the Muʿtazilites, "Humans for their part have free will and create their own good and bad deeds apart from God's control. God is therefore just to reward and punish. If God were the sole creator of all human acts, He would obviously be unjust to punish the unbelief and disobedience that He creates."[7] However, some of "their successors whole-heartedly embraced the determinism which they so earnestly wished to avoid."[8] The Jahmites, on the other hand, denied free will and adopted absolute determinism that ascribed to God the responsibility of what humans do. The Ashʿarite theological school believes both in human free will and in divine destiny and that everything happens by the will of God.[9] Islamic theodicy—which the Muʿtazilites, who were soundly described as "the most rational movement,"[10] and who pioneered its first arguments—seems to have gradually faded away as the Ashʿarites came to be the dominant Islamic theological school. As described by Mohammed Hashas (b. 1984) and Mutaz al-Khatib, "The case of the Muʿtazilīs is more than convincing to prove that even a religiously dominated context could bring about rational tendencies."[11] However, eventually, the Ashʿarites became the true representatives of mainstream Islamic theology and gained approval by arguing for themselves as providing a middle course. They summarized their argument the following way, "God alone created acts: man, however, 'acquired' these acts and so could be deemed legally responsible for his deeds."[12] However, instead of going over the details of the long history of debating this question, I suffice with reverting to my Qur'anic-based methodology to assert free will as a well-established Qur'anic condition and prerequisite essential for the human experience on earth as a divine succession, "Say, 'Now the truth has come from your Lord: let those who wish to believe in it do so, and let those who wish to reject it do so'" (18:29).

The second option is choosing to create beings that can but do not choose evil. What if human beings were created as beings who could still choose evil but were designed in a way that made them always choose and prefer what was good and righteous to what was bad and evil? S. Paul Schilling (1904–1994) argues against this option for being self-contradictory as he says, "we conclude that the notion of human beings created so that they would always choose the good is self-contradictory. If they were really free, there could be no guarantee that they would always choose rightly, while if they were so constituted as to exclude wrong choices, they would not be free."[13] While I disagree with describing such an option as self-contradictory, I still argue that this option is to be dismissed as applied to human beings. In fact, this option seems to have been divinely dismissed not for its incompatibility with human free will but due to its incompatibility with humans' divine agency. Human beings can still be soundly described as free—as long as they make choices—even if they were designed in a way that makes them prefer what is good to what is bad. One can have a multiplicity of choices that vary substantially but still share the attribution of being good or righteous. Or, put differently, one can still be soundly described as freely choosing even when one chooses out of one of many options that all share the quality of being good. Choosing to help a homeless person on my way to work, or back from work, is choosing between two options that can both be described as good. Human beings who can but do not choose evil do not lose their free will; however, they lose what is even more important: they lose the ability of choosing as a divine ability that they share with God. Because the type of ability of choosing that we share with God goes beyond the ability of choosing different tokens of the same type to the ability of choosing different tokens of different types as well, in our case good acts and evil acts.

It is important as well to remember that the choice to create beings that can but do not choose evil is not self-contradictory, because it is not a mere hypothetical assumption but an actual case.[14] In fact, this choice is the kind of creational choice that had already taken place when God created angels. Rumi describes angels as "abstract and free from lust,"[15] as he explains, "To be obedient, worshipful, and constantly mindful of God is their nature and means of sustenance. That is what they feed on and live by, like a fish in water, whose life is of the water and whose bed and pillow are the water."[16] Angels—as the Qur'an describes them—are beings that can but never choose evil as we read, "Believers, guard yourselves and your families against a Fire whose fuel is people and stones, over which stand angels, stern and strong; angels who never disobey God's commands to them, but do as they are ordered" (66:6); "The Messiah would never disdain to be a servant of God, nor would the angels who are close to Him" (4:172); and, "They are only His honored servants. They do not speak before He speaks and they act by His command. He knows what is before them and what is behind them, and they cannot intercede without His approval—indeed they themselves stand in awe of Him" (21:26–28). As al-Rāzī explains, "the majority of Muʿtazilites and many jurists believed angels to be capable of evil and sinning."[17] They used—as he explains[18]—for their claim the following arguments: first, what the angels said, "'How can You put someone there who will cause damage" (2:30), which can be interpreted either as sinning or leaving what was better to be done; second, the following verse, "If any of them were to claim, 'I am a god beside Him,' We would reward them with Hell: this is how We reward evildoers" (21:29), which textually asserts their accountability; and third, the verse, "[even] those who live in the presence of your Lord are not too proud to worship Him" (7:206), which praised the angels for leaving arrogance and thereby suggests their ability of arrogance, because no one can be praised for leaving a sin he or she is incapable of doing in the first place.

Humans' divine agency can't be fulfilled while lacking the ability to bring about evil; rather, it is fulfilled only by this unrestricted ability of free will, of choosing what is good and righteous or what is bad and evil. In other words, the ability of choosing good and evil is a divine ability that only responsible beings and divinely chosen beings like humans[19] share with God.

(8) God doesn't desire human evil by choosing to create beings that can choose evil and then by creating evil and allowing it as an option for them to choose from. Allowing only good and righteous outcomes to be chosen means banning and even eliminating evil from being chosen as an outcome. But eliminating all options and reducing all of them to one option, or one type of option, reduces the act of choosing itself into an act of accepting one forced option, or a forced type of option, that can only be categorized as good or righteous. Eliminating the ability of choosing by reducing choices into one choice, or one type of choice, is a violation of the status of humans as divine successors on earth. In fact, stripping human beings from their divine status can be done via either depriving them from their ability to make choices or by reducing their choices to one choice or one type of choice. To the contrary, we find both rights to be preserved in the Qur'an. First, free will is protected as we read, "There is no compulsion in religion" (2:256). Second, all options are made available to human beings to choose from as we read, "Did We not give him two eyes? A tongue, two lips, and point out to him the two clear ways [of good and evil]? (90:8–10). More importantly, and in addition, eliminating evil as an option results in turning human beings to amoral agents who may only choose from good and righteous options. Blocking evil choices and rendering them inaccessible turns all deeds and all choices, including moral deeds, into amoral choices. In a world where God allows only right moral

choices, there would be nothing to set them apart and distinguish from evil choices. In a world were evil choices are made inaccessible, there would be only amoral choices made by amoral agents. That would eliminate evil for sure, but that would eliminate good as well. Finally, such a place would be a world of one God and many puppets, not a world like ours—a world of God and God's gods.

(9) God doesn't desire human evil by choosing to create beings that can choose evil, by making evil choices accessible and then by refraining from deactivating the evil consequences of choosing evil. In other words, God is not evil for not intervening, in the last minute, once a human being chooses to do evil, by allowing the choice as a possibility while blocking its actual consequences. God apparently allows not only the evil choice but the actual consequences of the evil choice to take place as well. On might ask though: What if God solved the problem of evil by preserving both the human ability to choose and the existence of evil choices but then eliminated all evil consequences? In other words, what if the process of divine elimination applied only to eliminating evil and bad consequences? Wouldn't this option solve the problem? For sure, such an option would preserve humans' free will and their full ability to choose as well by keeping all choices—both bad and good—available. More importantly, this option might seem as if it could finally solve the problem of evil by keeping evil agents and evil choices while deactivating evil by eliminating evil consequences from taking place. John Hick (1922–2012) deals with this hypothetical case as he asks us to imagine a world in which "no wrong action could ever have bad effects, and that no piece of carelessness or ill judgment in dealing with the world could ever lead to harmful consequences."[20]

To explain more, Hick uses some useful examples:

> If a thief were to steal a million pounds from a bank, instead of anyone being made poorer thereby, another million pounds would appear from nowhere to replenish the robbed safe; and this, moreover without causing any inflationary consequences. If one man tried to murder another, his bullet would melt innocuously into thin air, or the blade of his knife turn to paper. Fraud, deceit, conspiracy, and treason would somehow always leave the fabric of society undamaged. Anyone driving at breakneck speed along a narrow road and hitting a pedestrian would leave his victim miraculously unharmed; or if one slipped and fell through a fifth-floor window, gravity would be partially suspended and he would float gently to the ground. And so on.[21]

Could such a world solve our problem of human evil? Hick answers no, because in that world,

> moral qualities would no longer have any point or value [. . .] If to act wrongly means, basically, to harm someone, there would no longer be any such thing as morally wrong action. And for the same reason there would no longer be any such thing as morally right action. Not only would there be no way in which anyone could injure anyone else, but there would also be no way in which anyone could benefit anyone else, since there would be no possibility of any lack or danger.[22]

In fact, this specific type of plan B or deactivation of evil that can hypothetically be launched by blocking evil consequences doesn't only cancel the act of choosing itself, through canceling bad and evil choices –the case I dealt with in (8) above—but cancels the act of choosing itself. This time the cancellation doesn't happen because only one type of choice is made available to choose from, namely, righteous choices, but because evil choices will turn to righteous choices due to the lack of any criterion to distinguish them from anything else. In other words, while case (8) means the cancellation of the act of choosing itself due to the cancellation of one choice or one type of choice, namely, evil choices, case (9) would merely constitute another cancellation of the act of choosing. This time, the cancellation comes as a consequence not of eliminating one choice, namely, the evil choice, but as a result of turning both choices into two identical choices or types of choice. The deactivation of evil consequences will simply deprive the human moral agent from any chance to view good choices as any better than evil ones.

(10) God doesn't desire human evil by choosing to create beings that can choose evil while knowing they will choose evil, because knowing something is not the same as determining it or bringing it about. But where does this illusion, which is created mainly by God's omniscience, come from? In fact, it derives from drawing analogies based on our limited epistemic abilities. It is an outcome of our human tendency to humanize God while we try to make sense of His unknown and incomprehensible attributes. As human beings we are not given foreknowledge. Therefore, one might be tempted to think that foreknowledge—if granted—can by itself change the future by providing humans access to it. At least—some might think—knowing the future can give us the chance to change what causes future outcomes by changing their current causes, either by manipulating the current causal chains, or by blocking the causal connection between current causes and future effects. In other words, connecting our knowledge of the future to the ability of changing it is what lies behind the illusion that knowing about something is the same as bringing it about. To dismiss this illusion of a necessary connection between knowing about something and causing it, it is sufficient to consider our knowledge of the past. As human beings we are granted an ability to know what had happened in the past; however, this faculty is distinct from

the ability to retrospectively cause things to happen or stop things from happening. God, by knowing about future evil, doesn't cause that future evil. In other words, God doesn't stage current causes to end up as future effects that He already knows; rather, He only allows the natural and causal flow of current causes to their future effects: God is not an active agent in the causal chain that connects the present to the future but a patient witness. This stance is documented in the Qur'an in many places. For example, in Q. 4:33 we read, "God is witness to everything." And, "Say, 'Wait if you wish: We too are waiting'" (6:158).

## THE PROBLEM OF "DIVINE EVIL"

My previous discussion of free will leaves behind many cases that the free-will answer does not address. Because, while free will explains but doesn't justify human evil, "divine evil,"[23] usually referred to as "natural evil," cannot simply be explained the same way. By divine evil I mean evil caused by reasons other than the human exercise of their right to make choices, both good and bad. Some relevant examples include natural disasters, pain, famine, earthquakes, epidemics, COVID-19 pandemic and so forth. Also, this includes cases of the unnecessary suffering of children and animals. As Andrew Michael Flescher rightly observes, "The ability to choose to harm rather than do good may be necessary to be human beings who are ultimately the best sorts of creatures, but goes no distance toward comparably interpreting hurricanes, tsunamis, and other natural disasters as goods without which we would be worse off."[24] I prefer the term "divine evil" to the commonly used "natural evil" because some cases of natural evil can be easily proven to be caused by human evil. For example, natural disasters caused by humans recklessly pillaging natural resources are nothing but cases of maximized human evil.

The problem of the existence of evil that exceeds what can be characterized as human-caused evil has been usually referred to as theodicy since Leibniz (1646–1716) first coined the term. As S. Paul Schilling explains, "The English word *theodicy* is modeled after the French in Leibniz's title, which is based on the Greek words *theos* ('God') and *dike* ('right,' or 'justice'). A theodicy is an attempt to vindicate the justice or righteousness of God in ordering or permitting evil and suffering in his creation."[25]

Jonathan E. Brockopp (b. 1962) draws an important distinction between pain, suffering and evil. "Pain is not always suffering and suffering is not always evil."[26] He explains, "For pain to be suffering, a particular set of circumstances is required, often including the loss of the ability to rectify the situation. What makes suffering evil, however, is the malevolent intent of others, which is perceived to be outside the bounds of acceptable human behavior."[27] "Deep suffering makes us noble,"[28] Friedrich Nietzsche (1844–1900) says. Friedrich Hügel (1770–1831) asserts pain as a useful human experience, "Since man cannot find his deepest by fleeing from pain and suffering, and by seeking pleasure."[29] But more radically speaking, for Hügel evil—as Peter Dews (b. 1952) explains—"is an essential moment, the 'negativity' that drives the dialectical process forward [. . .] a purely *transitional* moment."[30] Muṣṭafā Maḥmūd (1921–2009) argues for the existence of evil as inevitable for the "human virtue to exercise a role in resisting it."[31] Similarly, in his defense of the unjust and the uneven nature of what humans seem to be given by God, Swinburne refers to those events as a chance to give us "greater responsibility in the choices we make"[32] and as occasions and opportunities for us to grow in our character as moral agents.

> We are born into a world in which the good things of life are divided unevenly—by our genes, initially. Some are born so as naturally to develop into physically strong, clever, or beautiful people; others, not so. And society so often adds to the unevenness of the distribution of the good. The physically strong, clever, and beautiful naturally (unless prevented) acquire enormous power over others. The lame need help, but the beautiful command with a smile. There is no reason why a good God should distribute the good things of life evenly. If people contribute in some sense equally to a common enterprise, there is something wrong if they do not receive an equal share in its benefits. But if our creator creates us out of nothing, and gives to some ten good things, and to others twenty good things, no one is wronged; nor has he failed to be perfectly good. He has been generous, and, more so, he has made it possible for us to be generous. For the more power someone has and the more someone else lacks it, the greater the opportunity the former has to use his power to benefit the latter and above all to increase the power of the latter. If you are strong, you can use your strength to do things for me which I cannot do for myself. If you are beautiful, you can use your beauty to make me happy. If you are clever, you can use your cleverness to devise ways of making me clever. If we all had the same number of the same good things, there would be so much less scope for helping each other.[33]

Swinburne restricts this understanding of the right to use evil to God by saying, "of course, I am not saying that anyone other than God would have the right to allow such things to happen, without intervening to stop them."[34] However, the clear instrumentality suggested by allowing some humans to suffer in order to motivate others to think more responsibly about their moral choices is too controversial to be accepted as a moral right per se, even when limited to God. For example, interpreting the suffering and deaths of the Jewish victims of the Nazi concentration camps as a possibility that caused "a whole web of actions and reactions stretching forward over the centuries of sympathy for victims"[35] doesn't make the Holocaust sound more fair to victims and doesn't make God's choice sound more just.[36] Opposite to this line of arguing, I believe describing the Holocaust as "evil" is the least we can do to be just to the victims. Contrary to Swinburne, Sami Pihlström (b. 1969) pragmatically refuses "simple theodicist attempts to find fundamental order and coherence in the world"[37] and insists on acknowledging the reality of evil by saying, "a description of something or someone as evil may even be something that we morally speaking owe to the victims of that action or that person (which is obviously something very different from explaining those actions or the agents' reasons for performing them, let alone 'explaining them away' as evil)."[38] In addition to this concern, and as I mentioned before, this line of arguing allows humans to be treated merely as a means to an end, which contradicts the Kantian categorical imperative, "man and generally any rational being exists as an end in himself, not merely as a means to be arbitrarily used by this or that will, but in all his actions, whether they concern himself or other rational beings, must be always regarded at the same time as an end."[39] The fact that the end in this case is assumed to be divinely designated does not, and should not, allow for such a moral violation as long as the used subjects are rational beings and as long as "every rational nature is an end in itself."[40] In addition, explaining suffering by the later good it can bring about, in terms of provoking other humans to help and support the wronged and the less fortunate, leaves behind cases of unexplained suffering that do not even end with such a positive moral outcome. In fact, the mere existence even of one case in which human suffering does not invoke feelings of sympathy and human solidarity is able to falsify this line of thinking. One of the most glaring examples is the ongoing Syrian tragedy since 2011. The murder, torture, starvation, and displacement of hundreds of thousands of people cannot even be explained, let alone justified, if we take into consideration the world's shy indifference.[41] Solving the problematic aspect of ascribing evil to God by attempting at justifying it is a problematic approach that never reaches a satisfactory conclusion. In his critique to Hügel's conceptualization of evil as a "necessary moment in the actualization of Spirit,"[42] Richard Bernstein (b. 1932) says,

> But to affirm that evil is a *necessary* moment in the development of Spirit is to *justify* evil. Beginning with Hegel's contemporary, Schelling, and all the subsequent thinkers that I have interrogated—Nietzsche, Freud, Levinas, Jonas, and Arendt—there is a sharp critique of this Hegelian drive to an *Aufhebung* that heals the wounds of Spirit without leaving any scars. There are ruptures, breaks, wounds, abysses, and evil that are so profound that complete healing is impossible. There are wounds that do not heal, that cannot be sublated. There is *no* "After Auschwitz."[43]

While a project like refuting all and every attempt to justify divine evil goes beyond what I am more interested in achieving in this section, it remains as a fact that while the problem of evil "has always remained unsolved,"[44] "none of the classic solutions to the problem of the theodicy turns out to be completely satisfactory."[45] Although Isabel Cabrera suggests "not to try to answer the question, but to avoid it"[46] as "the best alternative,"[47] I venture out into another attempt by arguing for "divine testing" as what can explain divine evil. Divine evil does not exist per se. What does exist is divine testing, which should be distinguished from divine evil.

First, what is important to emphasize at the outset of this discussion is the negation of any direct logical contradiction—as some might think—between the existence of evil and the existence of God. There is no logical contradiction here, unlike claiming, for example, that God exists and does not exist at the same time. Or as Edward Wierenga puts it, "It is one thing, however, to question God about the presence of evil or to abandon trust in him because of it; it is something else altogether to appeal to the presence of evil to argue against God's existence. But this is precisely what a long philosophical tradition has done."[48]

Second, it is also important to remember that the problem of evil is a moral problem in the first place. It is not an ontological problem per se. Because the existence of evil doesn't contradict the existence of God; rather, it seems to contradict the existence of a just God. The dispute is not about the existence of God but about His moral character. Even if the argument ends by proving God as an evil deity, this argument by itself is not sufficient to nullify the argument for the existence of God. At the end of the day, the idea of God as an evil deity is not self-contradictory. Islam follows other monotheistic religions in asserting God as benevolent; however, it is useful to remember that some other religions adopted a less-appealing image of angry, hateful and even evil gods. What matters for us is the fact that those beliefs do not cause any logical contradictions or inconsistencies of any kind. In other words, the moral character of a deity, whether good or bad, positive or negative, is not essential in terms of asserting or denying the existence of that deity. The retrospective examination of some examples can reveal more. For example, Loki, in Norse mythology, is believed to be a trickster, a troublemaker, and a sneaky god. In Greek mythology, Zeus is portrayed as a womanizer who would do anything including disguising his own identity to seduce women. His daughter Aphrodite is portrayed as an unfaithful wife who cheated on her husband with many lovers. In ancient Egyptian mythology, the divine status of Set as a god did not prevent him from killing his own brother.

Third, evil itself is a mere moral evaluation. Evil does not have a clear-cut ontological status independent from the evaluating agent. Evil, for example, does not exist the way trees, rocks, and elephants exist. It is a mere belief that depends, for its existence, on an agent that has the ability of viewing and evaluating something or someone as evil. Therefore, the real logical contradiction is not between the existence of God and the existence of evil, because they can perfectly coexist; rather, it is between the two beliefs, namely, the belief that God is good and the contradictory belief that God is evil.

Fourth, "It is okay not to know why God does what He does." Edward Omar Moad explains,

> It is okay not to know why God does what He does. In fact, it is not our business. Our business is to know what God asks us to do, and then to do it. How do we know what God wants us to do? Certainly not by figuring out why He does what He does, and then calculating from that baseless speculation. God has sent His Messenger and His Message to convey to us in clear terms what to do. For example, He has said that we will be questioned, but He will not (Qur'an 21:23). Thus, we can understand that we should act under the awareness that we will be questioned, and should not expect from God an account of what He does. Then of course, do not pretend as if God has informed us of why He does what He does.[49]

We have seen so far that we can pinpoint a Qur'anic explanation of human evil, which is explained by the free-will argument. God, as we have seen, temporarily allows but does not desire human evil. He does that out of His respect to the divine contract with Adam and his offspring. However, how can we then explain evil in the world that goes beyond what I have categorized as human evil? Evil that cannot be explained simply as the unwanted outcome of humans unconditionally exercising their right to free will? Another explanation is definitely needed to shed light on divine evil.[50] In addition, an explanation is needed to bridge a huge gap in the free-will answer. Because accepting that human evil is allowed due to respecting free will leaves us with the question concerning the equal distribution of free will. In other words, in cases where humans cause other humans harm, how can we reconcile between the divine respect to the right of some to exercise their free will by choosing to harm others and respecting the right of the rest to choose not to be harmed? It seems as if the free will of some requires for its fulfillment the neglect of others' free will when they choose to be protected and saved. It seems as if when aggressors' free will is divinely respected victims' free will is divinely overlooked. The free-will explanation is not sufficient, then, not only due to its inadequacy when applied to divine evil, but even when solely applied to human evil.

In the following I argue that what can explain convoluted cases of human evil when directed against other humans, and what explains natural evil and all types of unwanted and undesired outcomes, is an understanding of evil as a divine test. Without inviting and implementing the concept of the divine test in our argument, all attempts to answer the question of evil remain incomplete. My Qur'anic-based argument for divine evil as a divine test is supported by the following observations.

(1) The question of divine evil is an unavoidable question. As humans we never start questioning evil until something disastrous happiness. However, the mere observation of the everyday inequality of distribution can prove us wrong. We don't really need—as some might think—an earthquake or a natural catastrophe to realize the existence of a problem. Evil is present the moment humans begin their worldly journey and does not leave them until its end. As long as people are born unequal—almost in every aspect—the question about divine justice remains deeply woven into the same fabric of our own existence. People are born unequal in many respects, in their looks, wealth, social status, health, and so forth. The gap that already exists once someone is born does not get any better, but keeps getting wider and wider as an affirmation of this inherited inequality, one that needs to be questioned and comprehended. Contrary to the many approaches to the problem of evil that sugarcoat the problem, I affirm the reality and the actually of the existence of evil. Evil is not accidental in our lives but existential, with no escape whatsoever; therefore, acknowledging its reality is the first step to overcoming it. To be clear, I have already dismissed the existence of divine evil and propose instead the idea of divine testing. However, this does not mean that evil outcomes do not exit. In fact, it is these easily observable outcomes that should motivate us to think of divine testing as the only explanation of divine evil. By "evil outcomes" I mean any undesired outcomes, no matter where we place them on the scale of undesirable experiences, either in our lives or that of others. What does not exit—as the argument is intended to prove—is divine evil that can be labeled as a cause that can explain evil outcomes by occupying the end of the causal chain. Evil outcomes are there, a reality that cannot be altered or improved by our denial. However, what lies behind these unwanted and undesired outcomes is not divine evil, which does not exist, but divine testing, which does. Also, I don't intend by my invitation to acknowledge evil at embracing it or giving up to it; rather, I mean adopting a mature attitude that can face evil in terms of understanding it first. Denying the existence of evil does not provide much help in terms of defeating it. Rather, it is the full acknowledgment of the existence of evil, and more importantly the full acknowledgment of evil as a test, that can help us better deal with it. This divine test, as I argue here, is eternal, mandatory, and applies to every human being without exception. The Qur'an affirms inequality of distribution as a divine test as we read, "It is He who made you successors on the earth and raises some of you above others in rank, to test you through what He gives you" (6:165).

(2) Simple and daily observations from life can assure the nature of life as a chain of ongoing opportunities to test humans. Worldly life is nothing but this continuous testing. Evil in our lives takes all shapes and forms. But only a close look at life can expose that evil, pain, and suffering are intertwined in all what can be described as a worldly experience. Evil, pain, and suffering include all unwanted events, obstacles, challenges, feelings, and outcomes. Indeed, the Qur'an refers to toil and trial as our essential human status and as what we were created for as we read, "that We have created man for toil and trial" (90:4). There is no room in (this) life for what can be called pure joy or ultimate happiness. The best one can achieve or hope for is to be content. Worldly hardship precedes, accompanies, and succeeds all and every step we take in life. It takes the form of the fear that anticipates any achievement. Then it accompanies all and every task or effort to bring something about when it takes the form of stress. Eventually, worldly hardship corrupts any genuine sense of pleasure when feelings of boredom and emptiness corrupt enjoying what we have desired to achieve. Ironically enough, all what one needs to lose a dream is to fulfill it! This is not to be confused with pessimism and ingratitude. One can always enjoy the moment, dream about the future and feel content about the past. However, unexplainable, passing feelings are always there as a reminder of the temporary nature of our worldly happiness and as a reminder of a lofty and eternal happiness that is still to come. As mere visitors on earth, subconscious feelings of nostalgia force us from time to time to compare all what we know to an unknown heavenly reality that we have never experienced! No mortal happiness can really satisfy immortal beings like God's gods on earth. Our unexplainable, existential longing to more than the temporary and the dissolving nature of our worldly happiness is an assurance that this worldly dwelling is not what we have been designed for as our final destination. It is true that some might feel totally satisfied and completely contended with life but that does not mean that they cannot at least imagine a better dwelling. We can always imagine and long for a healthy body without any fear of getting sick, an endless bounty without any chance of experiencing any loss or decrease, a youthful life without aging, and so on. In other words, there is always something better to long for. Our worldly journey is nothing but a test and cannot be what we deserve as God's gods. I am not to be understood as preaching for dismissing the so many joys and blessings we can enjoy in life—to the contrary, I am arguing for enjoying every minute and trying to get the best out of this worldly journey. What I am really arguing for is the assertion that, no matter how happy we can be in this life, there is still another meaning of an ultimate happiness God has in store for us. Unlike our worldly happiness, regardless of how perfect and complete this happiness might be, the happiness of the hereafter, which we can still at least imagine, is eternal, authentic, unconditional, never anticipated by

fear, never accompanied by stress, never proceeded by boredom, both spiritual and physical, and more importantly, it is what we can truly call "divine happiness."

The Qur'an keeps asserting the hereafter as the final destination by way of drawing meaningful comparisons between the illusory meaning of worldly happiness and the true meaning of real happiness preserved for the believers in the hereafter. Unlike all worldly pleasures, people in paradise never feel bored of their dwelling, and they never even imagine or wish for something better, as we read, "There they will remain, never wishing to leave" (18:106). Unlike the worldly life, believers in paradise can never be wronged or experience evil, "anyone, male or female, who does good deeds and is a believer, will enter Paradise and will not be wronged by as much as the dip in a date stone" (4:124). In paradise, the blessed do not have to deal with any kind of toxic or negative feelings, "and We shall remove any bitterness from their hearts" (15:47), or hear what they do not like, "Some faces on that Day will be radiant with bliss, well pleased with their labour, in lofty garden, where they will hear no idle talk" (88:8–11). Finally, in paradise the blessed will finally get to be reunited with their lost divine nature by reuniting with God Himself, "On that Day there will be radiant faces, looking towards their Lord" (75:22–23).

It is indeed problematic to try to solve the problem of evil in approaches that keep insisting on dismissing other closely related theistic aspects such as the existence of God, the Day of Judgment, and the hereafter. If the world is designed as an unstoppable continuous chain of worldly hardship, then an afterlife compensation is the only way to make sense of worldly pain and suffering.

(3) A problem that is closely related to my argument for evil as a divine test stems from the question as to whether the requirement of suffering as prerequisite for subsequent reward is fair in the first place. Can the reward justify the suffering? Why do we need to suffer first to deserve bliss afterward? If Adam and his offspring are not eternal sinners, as I argue in this book (see chapter 1), what explains, then, the need to suffer first? Does the later pleasure justify the earlier pain? One formulation of this objection is the following:

> The afterlife argument is far from convincing because it is very much like a torturer telling his victim on the rack that he need not be concerned for by and by he will be sent to a luxurious spa. To be sure, the victim is delighted to hear that he has such a future ahead of him, but he still cannot understand why he need be tortured before he goes. He cannot understand why the one should be a prerequisite for the other.[51]

The analogy the above objection uses doesn't address the core issues the afterlife solution really deals with. In the previous example, the victim is being tortured for no reason. In other words, whether the victim is tortured or not is irrelevant to sending him to a spa. The fact that the torturer decided to send him to a spa is not caused by anything the victim is doing or saying. In other words, the two events are merely correlated. In addition, the torturer has no right to put the victim in needless pain in the first place; the fact that he will be sending him to a spa doesn't make his torture sound any better, because by torture we understand a useless and unjust suffering. However, this does not apply to all cases of pain and suffering, for the above scenario is a case of useless and pointless suffering. Could we say, for example, that when a dentist causes his patient temporary pain, he pointlessly causes that pain to promise the patient a long-lasting relief of his toothache, one that can come only after and not before the treatment? Could we say that a math teacher who causes his students stress by testing them is torturing them by promising them the certificate after and not before the test takes place? Like these examples, and contrary to the spa example, hardship in this worldly life is not independent from the reward of the afterlife or merely correlated with it; rather, it is what leads to it, as asserted in, "'Peace be with you, because you have remained steadfast. What an excellent reward is this home of yours!'" (Q. 13:24).

(4) Worldly hardship and evil are not a fair punishment. Therefore, we should stop raising the question, every time the innocent suffer, as to whether or not they deserve it. In life, the good and the bad can be equally tested regardless of their merit. Are people fairly punished by evil? It might seem as a satisfying answer for some for the illusion of the immediate justice it provides. However, we should always remember that evil people suffer for reasons independent from their evil nature. No one suffers because they deserve to suffer. Evil people like good people may or may not suffer. Accepting the suggestion that evil people essentially suffer as a consequence of their bad nature or deeds leaves the question of the suffering of good people unresolved. I have previously criticized any approach that tries to solve the problem of evil while insisting on dismissing core theological elements like the Day of Judgment. This is especially true for this objection. As I have argued before, many Qur'anic assertions affirm that divine authority—including the right to judge, reward, and punish—returns to God on the Day of Judgment. No one is divinely taken to task for what he or she does before the end of the divine/human contract. In fact, contrary to a common line of arguing, people are not rewarded or punished for their worldly misconduct as long as the contract is not over. Instead of the argument for evil as a punishment, in the Qur'an we read about worldly evil as a way to motivate humans to repent to God, "We tested them with blessings and misfortunes, so that they might all

return [to righteousness]" (7:168). Or as in, "We inflicted years of drought and crop failure on Pharaoh's people, so that they might take heed" (7:130). We also read in the Qur'an about evil as a way to test the believer's faith and strengthen it; for example, Abraham's test:

> When the boy was old enough to work with his father, Abraham said, "My son, I have seen myself sacrificing you in a dream. What do you think?" He said, "Father, do as you are commanded and, God willing, you will find me steadfast." When they had both submitted to God, and he had laid his son down on the side of his face, We called out to him, "Abraham, you have fulfilled the dream." This is how We reward those who do good—it was a test to prove [their true characters]—We ransomed his son with a momentous sacrifice, and We let him be praised by succeeding generations. (37:102–108)

In addition, many times in the Qur'an—as explained in the previous chapter—worldly divine punishment is conditioned by an extraordinary interruption of the worldly causal chains. People are chastised only after an overt challenge is made to divinity and only after all worldly trial of humans loses its merit. Denial, after removing religion as a human test by deactivating all associated hardship, is what causes people to be divinely punished in the Qur'an—as fully explained in chapter 2. It is not the mere rejection of religion but the nullification of the human test after prophecies and miracles are demonstrated and after our experience of God turns into an empirical and evidence-based experience.

However, there are cases the Qur'an describes that might seem to be referring to evil as a worldly divine punishment, like the example we find of a town, "God presents the example of a town that was secure and at ease, with provisions coming to it abundantly from all places. Then it became ungrateful for God's blessings, so God afflicted it with the grip of famine and fear, for what its people had done" (16:112). Now, it is clear from the few examples we find in the Qur'an that there are some occasions when suffering, pain, and evil come as a worldly punishment. This poses the question: How can these cases be reconciled with my argument? Well, the mere existence of cases where evil people are punished does not suffice to make us think of those cases as the norm. Evil people might or might not suffer the consequences of their attitude or behavior before the Day of Judgment, in the same way good people might or might not be rewarded for theirs. In other words, people can be only occasionally punished or rewarded but are not necessarily and essentially punished or rewarded in the worldly life. What proves this argument is the many counterexamples in the Qur'an of unpunished evil attitudes and actions or unrewarded, faithful and good attitudes and actions. Let us consider the following examples: the Qur'an documents the previously mentioned story of the trench-makers, whom we know very little about except their horrendous torture of a group of believers in God as they burned them alive in a narrow ditch. Interestingly enough, the Qur'an narrates the scene without offering any action other than announcing God as a witness over what happened. "By the sky with its towering constellations, by the promised Day, by witness and witnessed, perish the makers of the trench, of the fuel-stoker fire! They sat down and witnessed what they were doing to the believers. Their only grievance against them was their faith in God, the Mighty, the Praiseworthy, to whom all control over the heavens and earth belongs: God is witness over all things" (85:1–9). In chapter 2 of the Qur'an, it documents crimes committed against messengers themselves as we read, "So how is it that, whenever a messenger brings you something you do not like, you become arrogant, calling some impostors and killing others?" (2:87). More importantly though, in addition to the many counterexamples of evil that is not punished in this world, the Qur'an literally announces the divine commitment to postpone all rewarding or punishing to the hereafter. "Do not think [Prophet] that God is unaware of what the disbelievers do: He only gives them respect until a Day when their eyes will stare in terror" (14:42). The same message is also asserted in, "If God were to punish people [at once] for the wrong they have done, there would not be a single creature left on the surface of the earth, but He gives them respite for a stated time and, whenever their time comes, God has been watching His servants" (35:45). What matters is the fact that evil as a fair punishment is accidental and therefore should not and cannot be viewed as the norm.

(5) The Qur'anic assessment of evil in the story of Job: any discussion of evil in the Qur'an remains inchoate without considering the story of Job. In this section, I discuss the details of the Qur'anic story. However, I start by affirming the morality of the story first. A big lesson we can learn about evil from the Qur'anic story of job is the following: we don't suffer because we deserve to suffer, we suffer because we are divine. Suffering as a test is unique to human beings. It is a demarcation of their divine nature. In fact, suffering and pain come as an affirmation of our status as God's gods on earth. There is no more self-loathing statement people can make about themselves when they think of their pain and suffering as an outcome of their sins or their bad nature. Similarly, there is no guilt trip more toxic than what can be caused by listening to those who justify our misery by making a reference to our human shortcomings. By doing that, human beings allow themselves to suffer twice. The first type of suffering is obligatory and happens with no prior permission, but the second type of suffering is voluntary. It happens when we internalize evil and think of ourselves as the reason of our pain and suffering.

The story of Job is an expression of condolence for those who might wrongly devalue their divine merit and accuse themselves for the pain and suffering they might face. Instead, feelings of pride for being divinely chosen for a hard test is what should accompany challenges of our worldly journey. The tougher and harder the journey, the more trust we should have in our religious and moral merit. Job, as the Qur'an confirms, suffered much travail, but his suffering didn't cause him to lose his trust in himself or to question his worth or morality. Instead, Job reverted to God as his refuge as we read, "Remember Job, when he cried to his Lord, 'Suffering has truly afflicted me, but you are the Most Merciful of the merciful'" (21:83). Job's cry was immediately followed by a divine response as we read, "We answered him, removed his suffering, and restored his family to him, along with more like them, as an act of grace from Us and a reminder for all who serve Us" (21:84). Reflecting on the story of Job asserts the following five observations about pain and suffering.

First, there is no mention of anything wrong or sinful Job said or did to make him deserve to suffer the way he did. Job, according to the Qur'anic criterion, was not a sinner who deserved a punishment; to the contrary, Job is described in the Qur'an as "an excellent servant!" (38:42).

Second, there is no mention of any remorseful change of behavior, belief, or attitude that Job had to go through before the suffering was removed. His cry and his prayers to God were simply accepted and fulfilled. This is another indirect conformation that Job's affliction was not meant to penalize or correct him or change his behavior.

Third, the story as the Qur'an asserts was narrated as a reminder for "all who serve Us" as the verse confirms. Job, according to the Qur'anic criterion, is considered, then, a servant of God and his story is narrated to all those who serve God as well. Pain and suffering can afflict everyone but especially those who serve God.

Fourth, God is the refuge from pain and suffering and not to be viewed as the reason for pain and suffering. This is quite the opposite of what some might say, think, or do when afflicted, as they turn away from God instead of turning back to Him. Understanding evil as a test that should eventually bring humans back to God is the key to accepting the challenge of evil, not for the purpose of embracing it or surrendering to it but to better overcome it. Job is described in the Qur'an as *awwāb* as we read, "He, too, always turned to God" (38:44). *Awwāb*, in Arabic morphology and as a rhetorical device, is the exaggerated form used to describe Job as someone who "*keeps returning* to what God commands."[52] The careful Qur'anic usage of the adjective *awwāb*, which is derived from the root *ā-b*, indicates continually returning to God as the original status of human beings, because, in its original acceptation, the root verb means to return, and unlike other synonyms indicates a return to the starting point.[53] It is the same meaning of a return to the origin we find in "It is to Us they will return" (88:25).

Fifth, for a better understanding of the problem of evil in the Qur'an, a clear distinction should be made between two verses that have been commonly but wrongly confused as referring to the same meaning or even as repeating the same scene. "The fallacy of exegetical semantic satiation," which lies behind such a line of interpretation, has been explained earlier in this book. These two verses are the previously mentioned: "Remember Job, when he cried to his Lord, 'Suffering has truly afflicted me, but you are the Most Merciful of the merciful'" (21:83) and "Bring to mind Our servant Job who cried to his Lord, 'Satan has afflicted me with weariness and suffering'" (38:41). Before discussing these two verses, let us reflect on the story as it is commonly narrated.

Mainstream exegeses provide a problematic account of the story of Job. According to many similar narrations, Job had a good life as a wealthy, healthy man. He had a big family and a happy life. His continuous gratitude to God aggravated Satan,[54] who challenged God that allowing him to afflict Job would reveal the prophet's hidden unthankful nature and eventually make him fail the test. After permitted by God to harm Job in all possible ways, Satan kept afflicting him with various calamities, first in his wealth,[55] then in his offspring,[56] and lastly in his health.[57] According to the traditional narrative, Job lost seven sons and three daughters in one day.[58] He lost his wealth, his health, and all his friends. After his prolonged sickness caused by itchiness, foul odors, and rotten skin ulcers, he had nobody left to help him other than his wife.[59] Nevertheless, Job did not lose his faith in God. Satan finally gives up on Job, whose suffering and hardship are eventually removed. Job is then miraculously cured, blessed, and praised by God as an excellent servant as he successfully passed the test.

Now, before reinvestigating the Qur'anic story a constellation of issues the traditional narrative suggests is to be considered. First, mainstream understandings of the role Satan played in the story of Job include a serious challenge to theological concepts deeply rooted in the Qur'an, such as God's divinity. As al-Rāzī explains, the mention of Satan as the one who caused the suffering of Job in Q. 38:41 was literally interpreted by many exegetes in a way that portrayed Satan as the one who actively caused Job his ordeal. As we have seen, many exegetical stories profusely narrate prolonged details on how Satan caused Job's sickness, poverty, and misery. However, as al-Rāzī points out, this literal interpretation was rejected by the Muʿtazilites for many reasons, including the issue of ascribing to Satan the ability of bringing about sickness and diseases, which would make him divine.

Second, this interpretation contradicts what God informed about Satan and his soldiers as we read, "When everything has been decided, Satan will say, 'God gave you a true promise. I too made promises but they were false ones: I had no power over you except to call you, and you responded to my call, so do not blame me; blame yourselves'" (14:22). Al-Rāzī, like the majority of exegesis, rebuts the Mu'tazilite criticism and tersely labels their rejection as "weak."[60] Interestingly enough, in his unjust attempt to falsify the Mu'tazilites' concerns and their insistence on rejecting any attempt to marginalize the Qur'anic text he commits the same mistake they pointed out by marginalizing the Qur'anic text one more time, as he claims—without any Qur'anic textual support—that Satan must have gotten permission from God to afflict Job! Regardless of this unjust attempt to undermine the Mu'tazilites' concerns, I argue that we have more reasons to accept their view than to reject it. Mainly because of the overt contradiction not only with the mentioned Q. 14:22, but also with similar Qur'anic confirmations like in, "Iblis then said to God, 'Because You have put me in the wrong, I will lure mankind on earth and put them in the wrong, all except Your devoted servants.' God said, [Devotion] is a straight path to Me: you will have no power over My servants, only over the ones who go astray and follow you" (15:39–42). Second, no textual Qur'anic evidence supports the mentioned details. The new hybrid story borrows from the Biblical narration without much citation. To avoid "excessive narrativization of the Qur'anic text," which can do more harm than good, I echo the Qur'anic minimalism here in referring to Job's suffering in such a general way. The Qur'anic story of Job when carried over in isolation from the Biblical story doesn't necessarily provide much unneeded details and unappropriated "exaggerations"[61] on what was the type, intensity, and nature of Job's suffering. What matters most from a Qur'anic perspective is the moral of Job's story and not the details. To be more specific, what matters most is his faithful, patient reaction to suffering and the way he resorted to God for help. While I limit myself to Qur'anic textual evidence in this book and eliminate any reference to hadith literature, or the Sunna, it is still relevant to mention that other than one hadith about Job we don't have any hadith evidence to support the detailed narrations we find about him in books of *tafsīr*. In this solitary hadith we find Job described as taking a bath when golden locusts began to fall on him.[62] What matters, for our purposes, is the lack of any textual support from hadith that exceeds the minimalist Qur'anic image.

Third, there is an overt contradiction between the story and the Qur'anic negation of any divine-satanic communication or his access to paradise after Satan was cursed and expelled. The traditional story of Job portrays Satan as overtly and verbally challenging God with his ability to seduce Job. In addition to lacking any textual Qur'anic evidence this claim elevates Satan's low status as an outcast and contradicts the textual affirmations we find in the Qur'an to any divine-satanic communication before the Day of Judgment. "Iblis said, 'I am better than him: You made me from fire, and him from clay.' 'Get out of here! You are rejected (*rajīm*): My rejection will follow you till the Day of Judgment!'" (38:76–78). Another Qur'anic confirmation that rules out the possibility of such communication can be found in, "We have adorned the lowest heaven with stars, [7] and made them a safeguard against every rebellious devil: [8] they cannot eavesdrop on the Higher Assembly—pelted from every side, [9] driven away, they will have perpetual torment—[10] if any [of them] stealthily snatches away a fragment, he will be pursued by a piercing flame" (37: 6–10). It is this difficulty that caused al-Rāzī, for example, to claim[63]—without any textual Qur'anic evidence—that Satan (*Shayṭān*) still had access to the heavens during the time of Job until this access was completely prohibited during the Prophet Muhammad's time.

What does the reference to Satan (*Shayṭān*) as the reason for Job's suffering in Q. 38:41 stand for, then? A meaningful reference to another opinion, which might be the key to unlocking this puzzling question, is made in al-Qurṭubī's commentary as he asserts that the suffering might be limited to Satan's whispering.[64] Ibn ʿĀshūr, in his interpretation of Q. 38:41, criticizes the many literal interpretations of the verse.[65] Instead, he refers to Job's suffering and weariness as an outcome of Satan's whispers. Satan, as Ibn ʿĀshūr explains, caused Job suffering and weariness by his attempts to make him lose faith in God and question God's justice in afflicting him. The other interpretation he suggests includes an implicit request made by Job for God to remove his weariness and suffering because of his concern that both would otherwise result in him giving in to Satan's whispers and temptation to blame God for his misery.

Now, having clarified the meaning of accusing Satan in, "Bring to mind Our servant Job who cried to his Lord, 'Satan has afflicted me with weariness and suffering'" (38:41), we can move to the distinction that should be made between this verse and another that seems as if repeating the same meaning as we read, "Remember Job, when he cried to his Lord, 'Suffering has truly afflicted me, but you are the Most Merciful of the merciful'" (21:83). While in Q. 38:41 Job refers to Satan as the reason for his weariness and suffering, Q. 21:83 doesn't include any mention of Satan this time. Thinking of the two verses as repeating the same meaning or even the same scene of Job complaining to God about the same thing overlooks the Qur'an's unique literary perfection where every sentence, expression, word, and even letter is supposed to play an irreplaceable semantic role. While many interpretations allow repetition of words and expressions in the Qur'an as a plausible linguistic option, made for the purpose of "emphasizing the meaning,"[66] Muḥammad ʿAbduh strictly criticizes overlooking the unique semantic function of synonymy in the Qur'an.[67] For him, synonyms in the Qur'an still have their independent meaning: synonymy, he argues, for the mere assertion of the same meaning does not apply to words in the Qur'an. I follow this line of argument, which I adopt myself to propose that Job in Q. 38:41 and Q. 21:83 is complaining about two different things. Or to put it another way, he was praying for two different requests in the two verses. Let's start with Q. 21:83. In this verse, Job uses the word *al-ḍurr* to refer to his suffering. In other places in the Qur'an—see Q. 10:12, 12:88, 16:53, 17:56, 17:67—the same word is used more generally to refer to any undesired outcomes one might have, such as poverty, fear, hardship, and so forth. The generality of the word, then, doesn't allow us to specify the suffering Job went through. However, what matters most is the confirmation in Q. 21:83 of the removal of his hardship, whatever that hardship might have been. This removal is ascribed to God Himself and is justified by His mercy. Also, what seems to be emphasized as well is the instantaneous response Job was granted as he sought God's help. This confirmation was made clear by using the conjunction *fa-* ("then," or "so") instead of *thumma* to connect his prayers to the divine response. *Fa-* as a conjunction in Arabic that usually connects two events without delay in time, is used in Q. 21:83 to denote an immediate reaction to Job's prayer and then an immediate removal of his hardship, which was granted once his prayer was answered. Now, while Job seems to be generally praying to God to remove his hardship in Q. 21:83, in Q. 38:41 he is particularly and precisely pinpointing a specific hardship this time. Also, he points to Satan as the reason of this hardship. By excluding the possibility that Satan could have actively afflicted Job, due to the concern I previously discussed and due to its logical contradiction with the rest of the Qur'an, and by excluding the possibility that both Q. 38:41 and Q. 21:83 could be repeating the same scene, by considering some previously mentioned exegetical views that suggested limiting Satan's harm in Q. 38:41 to his whispering, and finally by comparing Q. 21:83 and Q. 38:41—I conclude that Job was not complaining about the same hardship he suffered from as in Q. 21:83. Rather, he was complaining about specific mental and psychological pressure that Satan's continuous whispering caused him. Satan, who is completely incapable of bringing about any physical harm or causing sickness, was still capable of afflicting Job with toxic whispering and negative thinking, what we might associate today with anxiety, doubts, faith crises, stress, and destructive self-talk. Once again we don't have very many details to pinpoint the type and intensity of this distress, but at least we know that it was serious enough to force someone as righteous as Job to seek refuge from it with God. Job, who suffered as the Qur'an confirms, had to deal not only with pain and suffering but with a crisis of faith. He had to face what all of us can suffer once afflicted with pain. Job might have suffered from doubts and questions, as to whether he was suffering for a specific purpose. Perhaps he asked—like anyone in pain would—whether God was testing him or punishing him. In other words, Job was probably questioning the problem of evil itself, as would anyone who goes through hardship or pain. I support my conclusion by the following hermeneutical observations.

First, while Q. 21:83 points at an immediate and unconditional divine reaction that was brought about by God to remove Job's hardship, Q. 38:41 includes a list of recommendations that Job was given to deal with his anxiety. While I don't deal with the medical details and prefer to leave such research to people of expertise, I confine myself with a quick reminder of some suggestions made in Q. 38:42. The verse makes a reference to physical activity and cold-water therapy as we read, "'Stamp your foot! Here is cool water for you to wash in and drink.'" Hydrotherapy as a suggested treatment for anxiety and depression might be one suggestion for experts to investigate. I prefer this possible literal interpretation to a long exegetical tradition that inserted a supernatural element to the story without a textual support of any kind. According to many interpretations, a story of a miraculously healing spring of water was added to the main body of the story. For example, al-Suyūṭī mentions interpreting the order given to Job to stamp his feet as an order to strike the ground.[68] This striking of the ground allegedly caused a spring to gush forth. Allegedly Job was miraculously able to restore his health by washing himself in that water. He even added another spring that helped Job to complete his internal healing by drinking from. Interestingly enough, and contrary to this line of arguing, Ibn ʿArabī mentions Job's story in his book *Fuṣūṣ al-ḥikam* by asserting the importance of the water as what includes the "secret of life."[69] He also explains God's instruction to Job to use cold water as a way to treat "the excessive heat of his pain."[70] In addition, "weariness and suffering" in Q. 38:41 are figuratively interpreted by Ibn ʿArabī in a mystical sense as a reference to Job's pain for being unable to know and comprehend realities as they are.[71]

Second, another linguistic observation that one can draw from comparing[72] Q. 21:84 and Q. 38:43 supports my argument for two scenes and not one repeated scene described in both verses. In Q. 21:84 we read, "We answered him, removed his suffering, and restored[73] his family to him, along with more like them, as an act of grace from Us (*raḥmatan min ʿindinā*) and as a reminder for all who serve Us." In Q. 38:43 we read, "and We restored[74] his family to him, with many more like them: a sign of Our mercy (*raḥmatan minnā*) and a lesson to all who understand." As the above Arabic glosses in the two verses can reveal, Q. 38:43 justifies Job's help by God's own mercy. Q. 21:84 justifies helping Job by God's mercy but replaces *minnā*, which makes a direct reference to God, with *min ʿindinā*, which makes an indirect reference to God. This acute switch from *minnā* to *min ʿindinā* can be better understood if we trace the way both expressions are used in the Qur'an. While *min ʿindinā* stresses the source and locus of the mercy as divine—the semantic task accomplished by including the adverb of place (*ẓarf*) *ʿindinā* in Q.21:84—*minnā* in Q. 38:43 stresses the divine agency of God as the active agent in healing Job. This emphasis on God as the one who caused Job to recover is precisely deployed in Q. 38:43 to rebut any suspicion that Satan is equally capable of bringing about any tangible causal effects by himself the way God is. The precise reference to God as the agent in Q. 38:43, replacing *min ʿindinā* with *minnā*, brings the balance to a verse that seems to be referring to Satan as an active agent.

Third, while Q. 21:83 asserts the story as a moral lesson "for all who serve Us," Q. 38:43 asserts another lesson, addressed this time to "all who understand." If Q. 38:43 was merely repeating the same scene as Q. 21:84, how can we explain the switch of audience? In fact, asserting the two verses as addressing two different scenes can explain this change of audience. In Q. 21:84 removing Job's hardship was an outcome of his faith in God and an immediate divine response to his cry to God. Therefore, the lesson was addressed to those who can be considered an interested audience. Without a doubt, this scene is of interest to those believers who might find in Job a role model to follow when in hardship, and can therefore, learn how to revert to God the way he did. This scene cannot be possibly addressed to someone who has no faith in God in the first place, because accepting Job's prayer was contingent on him praying. Q. 38:41, unlike Q. 21:84, affirms a moral that can be of interest to an audience broader than the believers or those who serve God. This is clear from the suggestions the verse proposes of anxiety therapy that might be of interest to anyone as long as they suffer from a faith-based or even broader existential anxiety or stress. Believers and nonbelievers alike can suffer from mental and psychological distress and therefore the verse is addressed in a broader sense to those who understand.

Fourth, verses Q. 7:200–202 add to the evidence I have to support my interpretation for Q. 38:41. "If Satan should prompt you to do something, seek refuge with God—He is all hearing, all knowing—those who are aware of God think of Him when Satan prompts them to do something and immediately they can see [straight]." The previous verse uses the same verb *massa*, which is also used in Q. 38:41, to confirm Satan as the reason for Job's specific suffering. The general reference made in Q. 7:201 negates Job's suffering in Q. 38:41 as a case unique to him. More importantly, it falsifies the previously mentioned exegetical claim that Satan took permission from God to afflict Job.

Fifth, a clear confirmation of evil as a de jure test lies in the way the Qur'an ends the story of Job by a divine evaluation and assessment of the experience he went through. "We found him patent in adversity; an excellent servant!" (38:42). According to this evaluation Job is praised for his patience. The expression the verse uses comes from the root *w-j-d*, which means "to find." As we read in al-Rāzī's commentary, complaining to God about suffering and asking Him to remove it doesn't contradict patience "as long as one is satisfied by God's fate,"[75] because finding affliction desirable is not a condition for patience. It is Job's experience of evil, then, that made this divine evaluation possible in the first place. Pain and suffering, as the story affirms, are what God uses as an assessment method to check and confirm one's divine merit. Therefore, I argue for divine testing as what explains divine evil. As argued before, while the former exists, the latter does not.

Sixth, an investigation of the way the same adjective used to describe Job (*awwāb*) in another place in the Qur'an can help us understand Job's suffering more. In Q. 17:25 we read, "Your Lord knows best what is in your heart. If you are good, He is most forgiving to those who return to Him." In this verse *awwābīn*, the plural of *awwāb*, is used to describe those who return to God. But more importantly the verse makes a subtle reference to God's knowledge of what one might conceal. This reference to what one might keep in one's heart is deeply connected to Job's concerns. As I argue, Job in Q. 38:41 was complaining about a concern different from his concerns in Q. 21:83. In Q. 38:41 Job is referring to Satan and his continuous attempts to tempt him to lose faith in God. In other words, he is complaining to God and seeking refuge in God from his satanic-triggered, negative self-talk. Comparing Q. 17:25 and Q. 38:41 affirms returning to God and seeking refuge with Him from destructive self-talk, what one might secretly think of or even mental pressure as common to the meaning of *awwāb*. In short, the Qur'anic story of Job is a human application of how the problem of evil can better be comprehended and understood.

(6) The suffering of children: The suffering of children remains one of the most outspoken challenges to any theodicy or any proposed explanation of the problem of evil. In *The Brothers Karamazov* Ivan famously formulates the problem by asking,

> But then there are the children, and what am I to do about them? That's a question I can't answer. For the hundredth time I repeat, there are numbers of questions, but I've only taken the children, because in their case what I mean is so unanswerably clear. Listen! If all must suffer to pay for the eternal harmony, what have children to do with it, tell me, please? It's beyond all comprehension why they should suffer, and why they should pay for the harmony.[76]

Dostoevsky's Ivan in *The Brothers Karamazov* addresses the paradoxical aspect of viewing sin as an inheritable property when applied to children (even in a Christian context),

> The second reason why I won't speak of grownup people is that, besides being disgusting and unworthy of love, they have a compensation—they've eaten the apple and know good and evil, and they have become "like gods." They go on eating it still. But the children haven't eaten anything, and are so far innocent. Are you fond of children, Alyosha? I know you are, and you will understand

> why I prefer to speak of them. If they, too, suffer horribly on earth, they must suffer for their fathers' sins, they must be punished for their fathers, who have eaten the apple; but that reasoning is of the other world and is incomprehensible for the heart of man here on earth. The innocent must not suffer for another's sins, and especially such innocents.[77]

As we have seen in the previous section, human beings don't suffer because they deserve to suffer. Rather, they suffer because they are divine. The suffering and pain of children is not an exception. However, my previous argument for divine evil to be better understood as divine testing does not suffice by itself to answer the question of the pain and suffering of children where divine testing—if understood the same way as it applies to adults—is not even a plausible question to ask. Well, as I explain in this section while children do not share adults' responsibilities they do share with them in being divine. This is what explains their pain and suffering as I elaborate in this section. Contrary to adults, children—due to their divinity—are still tested with evil not because they can fail the test, but because they deserve the reward and the eternal compensation. As I argue, children have a unique type of divine testing, which, while rewardable, is exempt from punishment. If the souls of children are no less divine than those of adults, then there is no logical reason to be puzzled over the reason for children's suffering and pain. I argue for children suffering as a result of their divine status. Children are rewarded and eternally compensated for their worldly suffering. Children's souls are divine, therefore they are tested by pain and suffering. My argument is supported by the following Qur'anic observations.

First, in the Qur'an we read about a description of the final gathering of all living beings on the Day of Judgment. This gathering, as one scene explains, addresses the problem of the suffering of children by affirming the gathering and resurrection of newborn babies who were victims of infanticide,

> When the sun is rolled up, when the stars are dimmed, when the mountains are set in motion, when pregnant camels are abandoned, when wild beasts are herded together, when the seas boil over, when souls are sorted into classes, when the baby girl buried alive is asked for what sin she was killed, when the records of deeds are spread open, when the sky is stripped away, when Hell is made to blaze and Paradise brought near: then every soul will know what it has brought about. (81:1–13)

This important passage confirms the gathering and resurrection of all living beings including children and animals. The passage addresses animal suffering as well—as I discuss later—however, it is even clearer when it comes to the suffering of children. The verse in question (Q. 81:8) addresses a pre-Islamic misogynist practice, which gave parents in some tribes the right to bury their newborn baby girls alive for the fear of poverty or of the shame women would bring their tribes if captured by their enemies. This verse doesn't only assert the fact that children will be gathered and resurrected on the Day of Judgment, in addition it affirms the divine justice that will take place as the innocent newborn babies who were killed by their own parents will be given the opportunity to speak for themselves. Children join the hereafter, as this verse asserts, to be compensated for all the pain and evil they had to go through during their worldly life. The concern over the justice of granting a later pleasure when conditioned by an earlier suffering, which was raised by Madden and Hare in *Evil and the Concept of God*, can find its way to this argument one more time. Is it fair to require children to suffer first as a prerequisite for their later eternal happiness? In my previous argument I argued for the fairness of the earlier suffering when viewed as what leads to eternal happiness. In other words, the earlier suffering is what causes the later happiness and not only what accidentally precedes it. Likewise, I argue for children's suffering as what leads to their eternal happiness and not only as what predates it.

Second, if human beings suffer due to their divinity, how can we prove that children's souls are as divine as adults' souls? In the following I explain the Qur'anic account of children's souls. Clarifying this account can further help to unearth the reason children may suffer in their worldly life. The created human soul is referred to in the Quran as *nafs*. The term applies to the human soul starting from the moment of creation as we read, "People, be mindful of your Lord, who created you from a single soul (*nafs*)" (4:1). *Nafs* as the Qur'an describes applies to any living human soul that can live and die, "No soul (*nafs*) may die except with God's permission at a predestinated time" (3:145). Now, the term *nafs* applies to both children and adults. There is no reason in the Qur'an to distinguish between polysemous types of *nafs* that the same term can apply to. A clear Qur'anic law declares the gathering of every single *nafs*, without exception, as we read, "Beware of a Day when you will be returned to God: every soul (*nafs*) will be paid in full for what it has earned, and no one will be wronged" (2:281). The generality of the term *nafs*, then, which applies to children the same way it applies to adults, assures a shared quality or even a shared essence. It is this shared quality that makes children no less than adults when it comes to their spiritual status. Children are created the same way adults are; they are resurrected the same way as adults; they are as mortal and eternal as adults; and finally and most importantly, their right to justice is no less divinely preserved than that of adults. As the Qur'an confirms all human souls will return to God, without exception. In addition, every *nafs* will be given the chance to speak as permitted by God as we read, "and when that Day comes, no soul will speak except by His permission" (11:105) and, "That will be on the Day when every soul will come pleading for itself" (16:111). This includes children and even babies as we have seen in, "when the baby girl buried alive is asked for what sin she was killed" (81:8). The reference to this specific capacity of speaking and arguing should motivate us to rethink the full acknowledgment of children's souls. Children's worldly souls, as we can conclude from the Qur'an, will be resurrected as fully spiritually developed beings. In other words, the Qur'anic reference might be interpreted as an affirmation that no one enters eternal life as a minor or child. It is this full divine status that allows pain as a test applicable to children in their worldly life. No *nafs* is created by accident and more importantly no *nafs* comes to exist as a mistake. All is predestinated by God and all human worldly souls are granted equal rights the moment they are brought into existence.[78] Legally speaking, in Islam, children are exempt from moral responsibility until they become adults. However, this doesn't indicate any degradation of the sacredness of their worldly souls or diminish the importance of their existence, because they still have the same *nafs*. Therefore, when children suffer, they suffer due to sharing the divine nature, just like adults. Like adults, they come to earth as divine deputies. Therefore, they might suffer. Their pain is rewarded as they share with adults the right to immortality but their deeds are not taken to account. To summarize, children suffer, just like adults, because they are divine, the same way as adults. Their deeds are not taken to account, but their pain and suffering are rewardable. Children—at least from what we can infer from the few Qur'anic indications[79]—do not enter the afterlife as children anymore but as adults to enjoy their divinely granted immortality.

Third, children, unlike adults, are not to be considered legally responsible for what they do, one might argue, and therefore the same logic cannot and should not apply to them. Well, from a Qur'anic perspective, children are not tested the same way adults are, but they are still tested as divine beings. Or, put differently, children, unlike adults, cannot sin. But on the other hand, children are similar to adults when it comes to the full acknowledgment of the sacredness and eternity of their souls. It is this acknowledgment of children's souls as fully spiritually developed souls that allows children to share with adults in eternal life. Children, like adults, are fully eternally rewarded and compensated for their pain and suffering, yet they are fully exempt from any responsibility of what they do. The full spiritual development of children's souls doesn't make them responsible as long as they are children. The full acknowledgment of children's souls stems from acknowledging the divine status humans are granted as God's gods. This divine status—as I have explained before—comes from sharing God's own spirit, which applies to any human being, whether minor or adult, because it predates our worldly journey and is not contingent on any a posterior worldly biological advancement. "When I have fashioned him and breathed My spirit into him, bow down before him" (Q. 15:29). Children's souls are no less sacred than those of adults as long as they both share the same divine spirit. The full hereafter rights granted to children in the Qur'an are not to be confused with the Qur'anic assessment of children's worldly journey as gradual and periodical. Q. 4:6, for example, describes the age of "sound judgment" as the age orphaned children can be handed over their properties by their guardians. Another example is found in Q. 24:59, with reference to reaching "puberty" as a necessary condition required for children to be asked to behave like adults, by asking them to seek permission before they enter others' bedrooms or private places.

Fourth, the argument that children shouldn't suffer even to be eternally compensated because of their innocence doesn't apply to the Qur'an. As we have seen from my previous discussion and from rethinking the Qur'anic story of Adam in chapter 1, human beings don't start their worldly journey as sinners in the first place but as honored divine deputies on earth. Therefore, all human souls are considered innocent, including but not limited to those of children.

Fifth, the clear condemnation of killing any *nafs* in the Qur'an is an assurance of the divine status of the human *nafs*. "If anyone kills a person (*nafs*)—unless in retribution for murder or spreading corruption in the land—it is as if he kills all mankind" (5:32). This strict prohibition includes children, babies, and even unborn babies, like in the case of abortion, "do not kill your children fearing poverty—We will provide for you and for them" (6:151). Interestingly enough, the prohibition in the Qur'an does not distinguish any special cases as have been distinguished in schools of Islamic jurisprudence. Instead of discussing different opinions of cases in which abortion can be considered lawful, to save time and space I stay faithful to my Qur'anic research methodology and categorize all such proposals as non-Qur'anic.

Sixth, the Qur'an refers to a pre-ontological status that all human worldly souls enjoy before their physical worldly journey starts on earth. While very little is known about this mysterious, pre-existential, pure, spiritual status,[80] its mere existence should motivate us to rethink the equality of children's souls with those of adults. According to this theory, every human *nafs* experiences a type of existence prior to starting its worldly journey on earth. In addition, souls get then to be introduced to God and to acknowledge His divinity, "[Prophet], when your Lord took out the offspring from the loins of the Children of Adam and made them bear witness about themselves, He said, 'Am I not your Lord?' and they replied, 'Yes, we bear witness.' So you cannot say on the Day of Resurrection, 'We were not aware of this'" (7:172). While it is not clear if the Qur'an is referring to some type of innate and prewired religious intuition of some kind, what matters most here is the reference to the equality of souls in their pre-existential status. That is, before this concrete physical type of existence, known as the worldly existence, emerges. Children's worldly souls share the same preexisting form of existence, then—whatever this form might be. In short, because we suffer due to our divinity not because of our sins—as is commonly but wrongly believed—children who are as divine as adults can suffer as well. Both adults and children are tested by pain and suffering. While adults can fail the test, children are only rewarded and compensated for their submission to the Creator's will. No one enters the hereafter as a minor. And no one *nafs* is perceived in the Qur'an as less deserving of both life and eternity than any other.[81]

(7) The suffering of animals: if human pain and suffering is to be explained by free will when dealing with human evil and by divine testing when dealing with divine evil, what can possibly explain animal suffering? Animals do not have free will, and in addition, unlike children, they do not share divinity with adults such that the argument for their divinity could explain their pain and suffering. What, then, can explain animal suffering and pain? The many references to animals in Qur'anic stories make animals' unnecessary suffering a topic worthy of consideration by any Islamic-oriented theodicy. Animal suffering remains one of those puzzling questions that so many theodicies have just left behind, simply for the impossibility of applying the typical free-will answer to it. John Hick explains,

> A more moderate position, however, which would probably commend itself to most people, is that the organic cycle in non-sentient nature offers no problems to theodicy, but wherever there is pain, as there appears to be far down through the animal kingdom, there is a *prima facie* challenge to be met. On this view natural evil consists in unwelcome experiences brought upon sentient creatures, human or sub-human, by causes other than man himself.[82]

In his famous example, William Rowe uses the following case of the suffering fawn as a problematic case of pointless suffering:

> Suppose in some distant forest a lightning strikes a dead tree, resulting in a forest fire. In the fire a fawn is trapped, horribly burned, and lies in terrible agony for several days before death relieves its suffering. So far as we can see, the fawn's intense suffering is pointless.[83]

One closely related, tortuous difficulty stems from considering animals' moral perspective. We can always try to evaluate animals' best interests and what they might consider evil or good from a human perspective, but the impossibility of human/animal verbal communication invariably limits our analysis to a human assessment and evaluation. One can think, for example, of a general criterion like avoiding pain as a shared human/animal assessment of what can be considered as evil. However, the difficulty remains in the fact that whatever our moral evaluations concerning animal suffering might be, our evaluations cannot avoid "the mistake of projecting our distinctively human quality of experience into creatures of a much lower and simpler order."[84] At the end of the day, our moral evaluations about animals remain evaluations done on behalf of animals and not by animals themselves. However, the Qur'an provides many useful passages that we can consider for a better approach to animals' perspectives on good and evil. Sarra Tlili rightly describes this presentation as the most arresting feature of animal themes in the Qur'an. She explains:

> Perhaps the most arresting feature of animal themes in the Qur'an is the presence of the voices of certain nonhuman animals, which gives us the opportunity to see things—albeit briefly—from these nonhuman animals' perspectives. Obviously, allowing an ant or a hoopoe to speak in their own voices is quite significant, for in addition to familiarizing us with their viewpoints, quoting them directly tells us that they, and perhaps by extension all other animals, have voices worthy of being heard and views worthy of being quoted, thus showing in distinct terms the important status nonhuman animals enjoy in the Qur'an.[85]

In the Qur'anic story of Prophet Solomon, we read about one scene in which what is evil is described from an ant's perspective. "Solomon's hosts of jinn, men, and birds were marshalled in ordered ranks before him, and when they came to the Valley of the Ants, one ant said, 'Ants! Go into your homes, in case Solomon and his hosts unwittingly crush you'" (27:17–18). Interestingly enough, not only did the ant express what can be considered evil from her view, she used, as al-Ṭabarsī mentions,[86] the verb *udkhulū* ("*Go* into your homes") conjugated to address a plural rational group, instead of *udkhulī,* which is what should be used in Arabic to address a nonrational group. In the same chapter, we read about the hoopoe who came back to Solomon's court from Sheba and brought him news about people who worship the sun instead of God, "I found a woman ruling over the people, who has been given a share of everything—she has a magnificent throne—[but] I found that she and her people worshipped the sun instead of God. Satan has made their deeds seem alluring to them, and diverted them from the right path: they cannot find the right path (27:23–24). The hoopoe described what seemed unjust and even irrational to him by saying, "Should they not worship God, who brings forth what is hidden in the heavens and earth and knows both what you people conceal and what you declare?" (27:25). As Tlili elaborates,

> The perplexity the hoopoe displays about the people of Sheba's misguidance is another remarkable point. The fact that only God should be worshiped seems so obvious to this bird that it cannot understand how anyone could possibly fail to see it. Also, it is interesting that the hoopoe's statement suggests that its

> trust in the validity of its point emanates more from rational evidence than from instinctive knowledge that God cast directly in its soul, as the exegetes claim. The hoopoe argues that God is the only one who is worthy of being worshiped because He is the One who "brings forth the hidden in the heavens and the earth, and knows what you hide and what proclaim" (27/al-Naml: 25). Therefore, the hoopoe's knowledge of this divine attribute has led it to the knowledge of God, or at least to appreciate God's majesty and greatness. Being itself an expert in seeing what is hidden under the ground, as the exegetes agree, the hoopoe is particularly well situated to appreciate the divine attribute of bringing forth that which is hidden.[87]

But while this Qur'anic approach to evil as viewed from an animal's perspective clarifies some of the ambiguity, it complicates our argument even more by suggesting a level of consciousness parallel if not "superior"[88] at times to human consciousness! In addition, this Qur'anic approach makes the question concerning the justification of animal suffering all the more urgent. If human suffering is explained by people's right to free will, which they must have due to their divine assignment as God's gods on earth, what explains animal suffering? Animals are not chosen for any divine assignment the way humans are; they are not responsible; and more importantly, they do not have free will—yet they suffer like human beings and sometimes even more so.

To solve the problem of animal suffering from a Qur'anic perspective I propose starting by another question, one that concerns the final destiny of animals after the total destruction and perdition of the physical world as we know it. As we have seen in my previous argument, solving the problem of divine evil and human evil require the implementation of other theological aspects like the Day of Judgment. Likewise, I argue, solving the problem of animal suffering cannot be obtained without rethinking some animal-related theological questions. What would happen to animals in the hereafter? Do animals get to be rewarded or punished? Would animals be resurrected like human beings? Do animals have eternal worldly souls that can potentially survive the decay of their bodies? While so many human, egocentric theological accounts ignore many of these questions, I argue for the necessity of answering them as the first step to explain animal suffering. As we have seen, the Qur'an provides us a rare opportunity to view good and evil from an animal perspective. In addition to asserting some level of animal consciousness, the Qur'an adopts a puzzling biological egalitarian message when—generally and vaguely—describes animals and birds as parallel to human beings, "all the creatures that crawl on the earth and those that fly with their wings are communities like yourselves" (6:38). In addition, animals as the Qur'an assures live according to and in consistency with the divine will. In chapter 16, the Qur'an uses the verb *awḥā*, which is the same verb usually used in the Qur'an to refer to divine communication and revelation,[89] to name the way God communicates with bees as we read, "And your Lord inspired[90] (*awḥā*) the bee, saying, 'Build yourselves houses in the mountains and trees and what people construct. Then feed on all kinds of fruit and follow the ways made easy for you by your Lord'" (16:68–69). The Qur'an then asserts animal-divine inspiration. Ibn ʿArabī asserts animal inspiration as more approachable than human inspiration due to the former's "naïve nature."[91] Animals, as the Qur'an confirms, are taught how to pray and prostrate (*yasjudu*) to God and how to glorify Him, as we read, "[Prophet], do you not see that all those who are in the heavens and earth praise God, as do the birds with wings outstretched? Each knows its [own way] of prayer and glorification: God has full knowledge of what they do" (24:41) and, "Do you not realize [Prophet] that everything in the heavens and earth submits (*yasjudu*) to God: the sun, the moon, the stars, the mountains, the trees, and the animals? So do many human beings, though for many others torment is due" (22:18). The previous puzzling affirmations might be a metaphorical reference to their "submission"[92] to the divine will or might exceed what we can even conceive of or comprehend but can still assure the divinely harmonious nature of the biological world. Animals, then, like all other creatures—except for human beings—as described in the Qur'an share the quality of submitting to the divine will. Animals and other creatures (unlike humans) were not chosen, though, for fulfilling the divine assignment on earth; rather, they were created to complete the divine assignment solely assigned to human beings,

> He created the heavens and earth for a true purpose, and He is far above whatever they join with Him! He created man from a drop of fluid, and yet man openly challenges Him. And livestock—He created them too. You derive warmth and other benefits from them: you get food from them; you find beauty in them when you bring them home to rest and when you drive them out to pasture. They carry loads to lands you yourselves could not reach without great hardship—truly your Lord is kind and merciful—horses, mules, and donkeys for you to ride and use for show, and other things you know nothing about. (16:3–8)

This means that animals are created for a purpose. It might be different from the purpose human beings are created for, but they fit in the full picture by submitting to their intended purpose. Animals, as the Qur'an asserts, submit to God by way of submitting to humankind, who was solely "given dominion over the earth and its creatures as God's 'vice-regent' (*khalifa*)."[93] In Q. 36:71–73 we read about this special animal assignment, "Can they not see how, among the things made by Our hands, We have created livestock they control, [72] and made them obedient, so that some can be used for riding, some for food, [73] some for other benefits, and some for drink? Will they not give thanks?" It is this innate obedience of animals which allows for the "full human benefit."[94] In addition to this general purpose of helping human beings hold their divine assignment on earth some animals, as the Qur'an reports, are sent on special missions. According to a Qur'anic story, a group of birds was sent to defend against an army known as the elephant army. The success of the mission was documented in the Qur'an as we read, "Do you [Prophet] not see how your Lord dealt with the army of the elephant? Did He not utterly confound their plans? He sent flocks of birds against them, pelting them with pellets of hard-backed clay: He made them [like] cropped stubble" (105:1–5).

However, if animals do have a mission, if they are created for a reason and a purpose, and if they innately submit to the divine will as the Qur'an confirms—are they divinely rewarded or punished? In the following I argue for animals as eternally rewarded but not punished by God. My argument extends to provide an answer to the question of animal suffering. Animals are not assigned any divine assignment the way human beings are. Animals do not have free will and it is in their nature to live in accordance with the divine will by submitting to God and via submitting to His divine deputy on earth. The logical consequence is to negate the possibility that animals can be punished for what they do or what they fail to do. Animals, as Rumi says, are "under no moral obligation."[95] There is nothing that can be logically described as animal misbehavior from a divine perspective: dogs chasing cats, cats harassing rats, foxes hunting chickens, and so on, are all better described as amoral actions. In other words, sin is a concept unique and exclusive to evaluating what adult human beings do. At the end of the day, "sin results from the freedom of will that is an attribute of humanity."[96]

The real question, though, is one that answers the problem of animal suffering. Can animals still be rewarded for their spontaneous and innate submission to God or can they be compensated for the pain and suffering they might face? Rashīd Riḍā ascribed to the Muʿtazilites the belief in animals' resurrection that is held for "the general purpose of compensation, not for the mere specific purpose of punishment."[97] For the Muʿtazilites, as he explains, all living beings should be compensated for their sufferings and pain. If that pain was caused and decreed by God or His norms, like when animals are slaughtered to be eaten, or when other animals are killed to prevent their harm, then God compensates those animals for all of that. While Muʿtazilites, via their strict principle of *al-ʿadl* (justice), view animal suffering as an ugly (*qabīḥ*) outcome that is impossible to be reconciled with the belief in a just God, the Sunni consensus, as Abū Ḥāmid al-Ghazālī explains, views animal and children suffering as just, because injustice requires offending what others' own and, because everything is owned by God, "God has the right to do whatever He wants with what He owns."[98]

Unfortunately, while the previously discussed Muʿtazilite view—like the rest of their views—remains the less-considered and less-supported theological view, the many Qur'anic evidences I discuss support this view. As mentioned before, animals as the Qur'an asserts are created for a purpose and their submission to the divine will by submitting to human beings as essential for the fulfillment of this mission. Animals, as I conclude from the Qur'an, are not punished but are still rewarded for their innate submission; more importantly, they are rewarded as a compensation for the pain and suffering they go through during their worldly life. This conclusion solves the problem of animal suffering, because animals are rewarded for what they tolerate the way humans are rewarded for their patience. However, while we can refer to the suffering that human beings have to deal with as divine testing, we cannot apply the same term to the animal kingdom, because what animals are provided is a reward for their innate submission. Because sin is not a concept applicable to animals, rewarding animals answers the question from the divine justice of animal suffering. In commenting on the previously mentioned fawn case, Rowe asserts, "In the light of our experience and knowledge of the variety and scale of human and animal suffering in our world, the idea that none of this suffering could have been prevented by an omnipotent being without thereby losing a greater good or permitting an evil at least as bad seems an extraordinary absurd idea, quite beyond our belief."[99] Therefore, rethinking animal resurrection and the afterlife reward might be the key to solving the problem of animal suffering because an afterlife where eternal reward is maximized is for sure a greater good than any temporary suffering that an animal can go through. In other words, eternal reward in the afterlife is a case of a greater good that an omnipotent being allowed by permitting animal suffering, the case that Rowe described as absurd and beyond our belief. My argument for an eternal afterlife reward for animals is supported by the many Qur'anic textual evidences that affirm—contrary to the majority of what mainstream Qur'anic exegetes adopt—animals' final return to God and their resurrection on the Day of Judgment. The Qur'an literally refers to this as we read,

> When the sun is rolled up, when the stars are dimmed, when the mountains are set in motion, when pregnant camels are abandoned, when wild beasts are herded together, when the seas boil over, when souls are sorted into classes, when the baby girl buried alive is asked for what sin she was killed, when the records of deeds are spread open, when the sky is stripped away, when Hell is made to blaze and Paradise brought near: then every soul will know what it has brought about. (81:1–13)

Unfortunately, this clear reference to the final gathering of all beasts as one of the events of the Day of Judgment has been widely neglected or misinterpreted by some exegetes. However, many useful points are made by others. Ibn ʿĀshūr interprets the verse as referring to gathering animals in one place before the Day of Judgment due to a flood or any other catastrophic event that might force all animals to seek refuge in one place. He specifies this gathering of animals as an event that will take place during the worldly life before "the final annihilation of the world."[100] In the interpretation of Ibn ʿAbbās, though, we find a useful hint in reference to two possible meanings: first, the word *ḥushirat*, which refers to the gathering of animals, might be an indication of "their death,"[101] or second, it might be an indication of a final afterlife gathering for "retaliation."[102] Al-Qurṭubī in his interpretation ascribes to Ibn ʿAbbās affirming the gathering of animals on the Day of Judgment for the purpose of chastising the wrongdoers among them.[103] This process is followed, as he reports from Ibn ʿAbbās, by an order given to animals to turn into dust.[104] Al-Zamakhsharī mentions an exception to this mass annihilation of animals, which applies to animals that can bring joy to humans like peacocks and similar others.[105] Al-Rāzī in his *al-Tafsīr al-kabīr* ascribes to the Muʿtazilites the belief that the gathering of animals and beasts on the Day of Judgment "is for the purpose of compensating them for the pain they suffer from during their worldly life as caused by death, killing, and other reasons."[106] Once animals are compensated God chooses to keep some in paradise and annihilate the rest. Ibn Ḥazm asserts the final gathering of animals as a "doubtless" cogent opinion.[107] Indeed, investigating the meaning of the verb *ḥ-sh-r* used in Q. 81:5 and comparing it to the way the verb is used in the rest of the Qur'anic text can lead us to affirm the initial assumption that this verse is referring to the final gathering of animals as one of the essential events that will take place on the Day of Judgment. Unlike the view that Q. 81:5 might be referring to the death of animals, the verb is specifically used to refer either to the act of gathering or even the act of final gathering as we read in multiple places in the Qur'an.[108] What matters most is the fact that in all these verses, without exception, we do not have the above verb used to refer to death, which should suffice to dismiss interpreting the verb as referring to death in Q. 81:5. Next, it is also important to observe that all what we find to be supported in the Qur'an is the animals' final return to God as they will be gathered along with everything else on the Day of Judgment. All other details, like asking them to turn into dust, are mere exegetical additions with no Qur'anic textual support whatsoever. Another confirmation of the hereafter as the final destination for both human beings and animals is found in, "all the creatures that crawl on the earth and those that fly with their wings are communities like yourselves. We have missed nothing out of the Record—in the end they will be gathered to their Lord" (6: 38). As al-Rāzī asserts in his interpretation of this verse, "final gathering and resurrection apply to animals the same way they apply to human beings."[109] He ascribes to the Muʿtazilites the argument for compensation for their worldly pain and suffering as the reason for this gathering.[110]

The gathering and resurrection of animals on the Day of Judgment should motivate us the way it motivated the Muʿtazilites to rethink its rationale and reasoning. Now, the details on how animals would be eternally rewarded are not clear in the Qur'an, yet what is clear is their resurrection on a day divinely devoted for removing all worldly evil and injustice. Al-Rāzī refers to this specific point as a debated question. While the majority, as he explains, view this compensation as finite, which ends by asking animals to turn into dust, only a few view it as an eternal compensation, as he ascribed to Abū l-Qāsim al-Balkhī.

To sum up, what matters most are not the details about animals' final compensation but the Qur'anic affirmation that the animals' story does not end in this life. They, like human beings, still have another chapter to come. This is what explains animal suffering and pain. Animals are rewarded for their innate submission and compensated for their worldly pain and suffering. Animals are incapable of sinning; they are not assigned any divine mission the way humans are; they are not provided free will; and therefore, they are not divinely held accountable or punished.

(8) Equality of testing means individual assessment of testing: A big question related to God's justice is His justice in testing. If human suffering and pain is to be explained as a divine test that allows humankind to prove their unique divinely granted stature, the argument I adopt in this book, then God's justice in testing is a question that needs to be added to the list of questions we have to deal with. Inequality, as I argue in the book, is an unavoidable fact of life. It begins the moment we start our journey on earth and does not leave us until we end this journey. This simple observation suggests the question: How would people be judged, then? If some are given easy challenges and some are given hard challenges, how is it fair to ask them to be equally patient and devout? What complicates this question even more are simple details related to our journey on earth, which might look as if contradicting any equality involved in testing. For example, test practices include among other conditions providing tested students the same questions, and allowing them the same training and testing time—at least for students with no certified disabilities—and the same grading scale. Nothing of the previously mentioned applies to our worldly pain and suffering. Humans vary in how long they live, in the training opportunities they are provided with for better spirituality and religiosity, and in the amount of encouragement they get. They face variable challenges and they get variable support and sometimes they don't get any support from others. For example, how can someone who is raised in a religious or moral family that reinforces and encourages all

and every moral behavior be compared to someone who finds themselves on the streets and has no body to provide them shelter, support, or even love and sympathy? More importantly, how can both be required or expected to behave in the same way? How can someone who lost their child to cancer be expected not to lose their faith in God the same way one who did not have to undergo that challenge? Questions of this type are almost endless. But some can turn to address the core concept of religion itself. What about people who were not adequately introduced to any positive image of God? Many, if not the overriding majority of, adherents of every religion find it totally rational to variably adopt an exclusive approach that labels every other religion as false. However, finding counterexamples not out of those who intentionally reject their faith but out of those who simply didn't get the privilege of being introduced to it is not an impossible task. It is logically possible to think of individuals or even communities who have lived or are still living remotely with no access to divine salvation. In a previous argument in chapter 2, I made reference to the specific meaning that unbelief carries in the Qur'an. I explained how ignorance of truth doesn't count as an active rejection of it. Only those who recognize a certain truth as a truth and then freely and rationally decide to deny it can count as unbelievers from a Qur'anic perspective. However, this observation doesn't address the current problem of the inequality in testing. In fact, the key to understanding the Qur'anic philosophy of testing starts by replacing the concept of equality with the concept of equity and by replacing the idea of collective testing with individual and customized testing. In a race where people start from different places or times no definite ending time or place can demark, evaluate, or compare their achievement. Inequality in life necessitates testing as individual and incomparable. It is essential to keep in mind the strict three-dimensional concept of human responsibility in the Qur'an for any hope of unfolding the true status humans have on earth as God's gods.

First, human responsibility in the Qur'an is idiosyncratic. In Q. 19:95 we read a confirmation of the final individual judgment, "He has counted them all: He has numbered them exactly—and they will each return to Him on the Day of Resurrection all alone."

Second, human responsibility is individual. As the Qur'an makes it clear, there is no "follower" excuse that can pardon one from one's full share of responsibility. The Qur'an condemns blind obedience to traditions and ancestors and prioritizes instead the appeal to reason over the appeal to authority as we read, "Most of them do not use reason: when it is said to them, 'Come to what God has sent down, and to the Messenger,' they say, 'What we inherited from our forefathers is good enough for us,' even though their forefathers knew nothing and were not guided" (5:103–104). There is no excuse even for following others in their beliefs or acts out of persecution. This is clear in,

"When the angels take the souls of those who have wronged themselves, they ask them, 'What circumstances were you in?' They reply, 'We were oppressed in this land,' and the angels say, 'But was God's earth not spacious enough for you to migrate to some other places?' These people will have Hell as their refuge, and evil destination, but not so the truly helpless men, women, and children who have no means in their power nor any way to leave" (4:97–98).

Finally, human responsibility in a Qur'anic sense, as has been explained before, is indivisible. This is essential to keep in mind, because many theodicies have no problem accepting full human responsibility in cases of minor human evil but then switch to rejecting human responsibility in cases of tragedies and mass acts of human evil. In the Qur'an the acknowledgment of the existence of evil does not necessitate an immediate response, because that would violate humans' full responsibility. "Do not think [Prophet] that God is unaware of what the disbelievers do: He only gives them respite until a Day when their eyes will stare in terror" (14:42).

By comparing ourselves to others in their religious merit we commit two mistakes: first, we assume equality in outcomes, which overlooks the missing equality in conditions and prerequisites. In the Qur'an final judgment is strictly described as an individual and personal judgment. Had the same testing for adherents of the same religions or doctrines been recognized, this reference to individuals would have been needless. According to the Qur'an people are not judged as groups, rather they are judged as individuals. "That will be on the Day when every soul (*nafs*) will come pleading for itself, when every soul (*nafs*) will be paid in full for all its actions and they will not be wronged" (16:111). Second, we invade a divine prerogative preserved exclusively to God as "the Judge" as we read in, "on the Day when God will raise everyone and make them aware of what they have done. God has taken account of it all, though they may have forgotten: He witnesses everything" (58:6). Any religious-based merit assessed by anyone other than God is essentially misleading and erroneous.

(9) Reconciling the contradictory free will of different human beings: If all human beings are equally divinely granted an unconditional right to free will, how can we explain conflicts of interest of free will? If an offender's free will allows him or her to act as an aggressor, what about the free will of the victim, who desires not to be harmed? As I mentioned before, there is a gap in the free-will explanation that can only be filled by understanding the concept of evil as a divine test. Chapter 83 of the Qur'an, for example, draws a contrast between the blessed life believers enjoy in the hereafter and the evil they have to deal with in their worldly journey. There are two things we can easily conclude from this chapter: first, the bad behavior of those who bullied and ridiculed believers in the worldly life was neither punished nor corrected before the Day of Judgment; and second, the reward of the hereafter

does not only follow worldly commitment and faithfulness but is caused by both, even at times when demonstrating this commitment means dealing with pain and suffering.

> The truly good will live in bliss, seated on couches, gazing around. You will recognize on their faces the radiance of bliss. They will be served a sealed nectar, its seal [performed with] a fragrant herb—let those who strive, strive for this—mixed with the water of Tasnim, a spring from which those brought near will drink. The wicked used to laugh at the believers—they would wink at one another when the believers passed by them, joke about them when they got back to their own people, and say, when they saw them, "These people are misguided," though they were not sent to be their keepers—so today the believers are laughing at the disbelievers as they sit on couches, gazing around. Have the disbelievers [not] been repaid for their deeds? (83:22–36)

(10) The rebellious assertion of God as the source of all and every evil has no credibility other than its psychological appeal: Richard Bernstein rightly says, "Even when we think we have abandoned the search for essences, there is something uncanny about the way in which this desire and need expresses themselves in devious ways, this is especially evident in the discourse about evil. There is something deep in us that desires a reassuring closure. "[111] I opened the book by arguing against the illusion of a bad start that we had as humans on earth. Another illusion, which is no less serious and erroneous than the first, is the illusion of a guaranteed worldly happy ending. The need and desire for finding answers and the hope for worldly justice is not promised anywhere in the Qur'an, nor in any other religious books. More seriously, even our common sense and everyday life events contradict thinking of happy endings as the norm. Yet, driven by a pure psychological desire we keep searching for satisfactory answers, we keep hoping for guaranteed happy endings, and we blame God for promises of pure worldly happiness, endless abundance, and divine justice that He never made.

But what explains this counterintuitive human nostalgia, of a missing worldly divine justice that was never promised in scripture and never manifests itself as a reality? The human yearning for genuine divine justice in this world is immature and does more psychological harm than good. In spite of their illusory appeal, happy endings are as random and arbitrary as deplorable endings. Good and bad people equally suffer regardless of their moral and ethical merit. Instead of unleashing this insatiable desire to fix what keeps challenging us in an unfixable reality, accepting such a harsh and dreadful truth and embracing the challenge as a "test" provides better chances of dealing with reality and coping with its unpredictable nature. Like Said Mahran in the famous *The Thief and the Dogs*,[112] who got out of prison, not to start a new chapter in his life, but to go after the rest of the "dogs" who betrayed him in and out of prison, we lose even more by obsessing over a utopian concept of worldly justice. Said Mahran lost his chance to start a new life twice, first by his friends, "the dogs" who betrayed him, and second by the police "dogs" while he was trying to correct what he viewed as evil. Similar to Said Mahran we lose, not once but twice, if we keep whining worldly evil and denying its existence.

As much as it might be psychologically appealing to think of a permanent shelter, guaranteed happy endings, and stories that all end by defeated adversaries and triumphant protagonists, the appeal of such a line of thinking lies only in its illusory efficacy in terms of avoiding responsibility. In fact, it is what lies beneath our human impatience with worldly evil and injustice. But more importantly, it is what provides a pseudo-relief by avoiding our burden of responsibility as God's gods on earth. Accusing an all-powerful deity, who is supposed to wave his magic wand every time someone messes up to correct the outcomes of their actions, is for sure way easier than standing up to take full responsibility for what we do and what we fail to do. Unlike many, Voltaire faced the problem straightforwardly as he "placed the responsibility for the world entirely in man's hands."[113] In Voltaire's (1694–1778) satire *Candide*, James meaningfully says, "Mankind have a little corrupted nature, for they were not born wolves; God has given them neither cannon of four-and-twenty pounders, nor bayonets; and yet they have made cannon and bayonets to destroy one another."[114] As Richard E. Singer explains,

> Voltaire thus rejected the idea that a "creating" God, a God who formed the world and man, managed to establish the best of all possible worlds. He did not. In Voltaire's thinking, God left this opportunity to man. It was man's duty to himself to make of his world more than it was when he found it. In progress there was greatest opportunity for human expression and human fulfillment.[115]

Sartre takes this acknowledgment of human responsibility to the next level as he says, "And when we say that a man is responsible for himself, we do not only mean that he is responsible for his own individuality, but that he is responsible for all men."[116] While I don't follow atheistic existentialism in denying the existence of God, reclaiming our divine status as God's gods on earth meets with the existential wake-up call to stand up for our responsibility in acting to conquer and eradicate evil. Living up to our responsibilities as God's gods on earth is for sure a terrifying task that we are ready almost to do anything to deny or suppress.

In addition to demonizing God for not living up to our unrealistic expectations of fairness and justice in worldly life, another refuge is commonly sought in salvific characters that different cultures and religions keep fantasizing about as an outlet to escape dealing with reality as a test divinely designed by God for God's gods to reclaim their divinity. Chapter 4 is devoted to discussing the human yearning for closure and avoidance of individual responsibility as manifested in Islamic apocalyptic literature.

## NOTES

1. David Hume, *Dialogues concerning Natural Religion* (Raleigh, NC: Generic NL Freebook Publisher), 68, http://search.ebscohost.com.libproxy.unl.edu/login.aspx?direct=true&db=nlebk&AN=1085903&site=ehost-live.

2. Richard Swinburne, *Providence and the Problem of Evil* (New York: Oxford University Press, 1998), 127.

3. Joey Green, *Jesus and Muhammad: The Parallel Sayings* (Berkeley, CA: Seastone, 2003), 147.

4. Muḥammad Zīnū, *Rasā'il al-tawjihāt al-Islāmiyya* (Riyadh: al-Sumiʿī, 1997), 2:163.

5. Peter Green, *The Problem of Evil* (London: Longmans, Green and Co., 1920), 61.

6. David Birnbaum, *God and Evil* (Hoboken, NJ: Ktav Publishing House, 1989), 156.

7. Jon Hoover, *Ibn Taymiyya's Theodicy of Perpetual Optimism* (Leiden: Brill, 2007), 2.

8. William Lane Craig, *The Kalām Cosmological Argument* (London: Palgrave Macmillan, 1979), 6.

9. al-Rāzī, *al-Tafsīr al-kabīr*, 21:110.

10. Peter R. Demant, *Islam vs. Islamism* (London: Praeger, 2006), 14.

11. Mohammed Hashas and Mutaz al-Khatib. Introduction in, Islamic Ethics and the Trusteeship Paradigm: Taha Abderrahmane's Philosophy in Comparative Perspectives, edited by Mohammed Hashas and Mutaz al-Khatib (Brill, 2020), 3.

12. Eric L. Ormsby, *Theodicy in Islamic Thought: The Dispute over al-Ghazālī's "Best of All Possible Worlds"* (Princeton, NJ: Princeton University Press, 1984), 24.

13. S. Paul Schilling, *God and Human Anguish* (Nashville: Abingdon, 1977), 209.

14. For the theist.

15. Rumi, *Signs of the Unseen*, 81.

16. Ibid.

17. al-Rāzī, *al-Tafsīr al-kabīr*, 2:186.

18. Ibid.

19. And jinn. This other option, however, exceeds the limit of my discussion.

20. John Hick, *Evil and the God of Love* (London: Macmillan, 1977), 324.

21. Ibid.

22. Ibid., 324–25.

23. I am loosely using this term so far. Eventually, this term is to be rejected and replaced by "divine testing."

24. Andrew Michael Flescher, *Moral Evil* (Washington, DC: Georgetown University Press, 2013), 99.

25. Schilling, *God and Human Anguish*, 55.

26. Jonathan E. Brockopp, "Islam" In *Evil and Suffering*, ed. Jacob Neusner (Eugene, OR: Wipf and Stock, 2007), 122.

27. Ibid, 120.

28. Nietzsche, *Beyond Good and Evil*, 167.

29. Friedrich Hügel, *Essays & Addresses on the Philosophy of Religion* (London: Dent, 1963 [1921]), 111.

30. Peter Dews, *The Idea of Evil* (Malden, MA: Wiley-Blackwell: 2008), 89.

31. Muṣṭafā Maḥmūd, *Allāh* (Cairo: Akhbār al-Yawm, 2001), 92.

32. Swinburne, *Providence and the Problem of Evil*, 151.

33. Ibid., 149.

34. Ibid., 151.

35. Ibid.

36. This is the example Swinburne uses. According to my argument, the Holocaust is an example for human evil that God allows but doesn't desire. More importantly, it is a human evil that can be explained but can't be justified.

37. Sami Pihlström, *Pragmatic Pluralism and the Problem of God* (New York: Fordham University Press), 154.

38. Ibid., 141.

39. Immanuel Kant, *Fundamental Principles of the Metaphysics of Morals*, trans. Thomas Kingsmill Abbott (Raleigh, NC: Generic NL Freebook Publisher), 32, http://search.ebscohost.com.libproxy.unl.edu/login.aspx?direct=true&db=nlebk&AN=1085903&site=ehost-live.

40. Ibid., 34.

41. According to my argument, this is another example of human evil that can only by explained but not justified.

42. Richard Bernstein, *Radical Evil: A Philosophical Interrogation* (Cambridge, MA: Blackwell Publishers Inc., 2002), 229.

43. Ibid.

44. Tubanur Yesilhark Ozkan, *A Muslim Response to Evil: Said Nursi on the Theodicy: Contemporary Thought in the Islamic World* (New York: Routledge, 2016), 195.

45. Isabel Cabrera, "Is God Evil?" in *Rethinking Evil*, ed. Maria Pia Lara (Berkeley, CA: University of California Press, 2001), 21.

46. Ibid.

47. Ibid. According to her suggestion, the problem lies in the anthropomorphic language the majority of religious texts use to speak of God. This personalizing language, which allows for holding God responsible for an evil as a moral character, she argues, should not exceed from "speaking to God" to "speaking about God."

48. Edward Wierenga, *The Philosophy of Religion* (Chichester, UK: Wiley-Blackwell, 2016), 51.

49. Edward Omar Moad, "It's Okay Not to Know God's Plan," Yaqeen Institute, November 5, 2020, accessed 4/17/2021, https://yaqeeninstitute.org/edward-omar-moad/its-okay-not-to-know-gods-plan.

50. I will be loosely using this expression although I have already dismissed the existence of "divine evil." Eventually, what does exist is "divine testing" and not divine evil.

51. Edward H. Madden and Peter H. Hare, *Evil and the Concept of God* (Springfield, IL: Charles C. Thomas, 1968), 65.

52. Ibn ʿĀshūr, *al-Taḥrīr wa-l-tanwīr*, 23:227 (emphasis added).

53. Abū Hilāl al-ʿAskarī, *al-Furūq al-lughawiyya* (Beirut: Dār al-Kutub al-ʿIlmiyya, 2000), 339.

54. The Devil is referred to as Satan (Ar. *Shayṭān*) in this story as he should be named in his earthly transformation as I have discussed previously.

55. al-Rāzī, *al-Tafsīr al-kabīr*, 22:204.

56. Ibid., 205.

57. Ibid.

58. Ibn ʿĀshūr, *al-Taḥrīr wa-l-tanwīr*, 17:126.

59. al-Rāzī, *al-Tafsīr al-kabīr*, 22:205.

60. Ibid., 208.

61. Ibn ʿĀshūr, *al-Taḥrīr wa-l-tanwīr*, 17:126.

62. al-Bukhārī, *Ṣaḥīḥ al-Bukhārī*, 78 (hadith no. 279).

63. al-Rāzī, *al-Tafsīr al-kabīr*, 22:204.

64. al-Qurṭubī, *al-Jāmiʿ li-aḥkām al-Qurʾān*, 18:211.

65. Ibn ʿĀshūr, *al-Taḥrīr wa-l-tanwīr*, 23:270.

66. Abū ʿAbd Allāh Muḥammad b. Abī Bakr b. Ayyūb Ibn Qayyim al-Jawziyya, *Kitāb al-Fawāʾid al-mushawwiq ilā ʿulūm al-Qurʾān wa-ʿilm al-bayān* (Cairo: Maṭbaʿat al-Saʿāda, 1909), 111.

67. Muḥammad ʿAbduh, *Durūs min al-Qurʾān* (Cairo: Dār al-Hilāl, 1959), 55.

68. al-Suyūṭī, *al-Durr al-manthūr*, 10:344.

69. Abū ʿAbd Allāh Muḥyī al-Dīn Ibn ʿArabī, *Fuṣūṣ al-ḥikam*, with notes by Abū al-ʿUlā ʿAfīfī (Beirut: Dār al-Kitāb al-ʿArabī, 1946), 170.

70. Ibid., 171.

71. Ibid., 173.

72. I am adding some parts in Arabic, because the English translation doesn't show the subtle use of similar expressions in the two verses.

73. I don't agree with rendering *ātaynāhu* as "to restore," because this is an interpretive translation not true to the verb. I would propose "to give" instead. As the verse suggests, at the end of the day all the stories about Job's loss of his family might not be that credible. Probably, Job was blessed with a family after and not before his hardship was removed. In other words, his family was not replaced later on, rather he was given a family later on. This interpretation which fits more the verb the verse uses matches also the basics concerning human psychology. No one really can replace diseased family members or compensate for their absence.

74. The same concern applies here as well. The verb is best translated as "to bestow."

75. al-Rāzī, *al-Tafsīr al-kabīr*, 22:209.

76. Fyodor Dostoevsky, *The Brothers Karamazov*, trans. Garnett Constance (Grand Rapids, MI: Generic NL Freebook Publisher), 164, http://search.ebscohost.com.libproxy.unl.edu/login.aspx?direct=true&db=nlebk&AN=2009162&site=ehost-live.

77. Ibid., 160.

78. This applies to the *nafs* of unborn babies.

79. Like the previously mentioned ability of speaking and arguing ascribed to newborn victims of infanticide. See Q. 81:8.

80. I stay strict to the little we know about this from the Qur'an and avoid a log exegetical discussion of what is commonly referred to as *ʿālam al-dharr*.

81. I confine myself to this underdeveloped discussion of the underestimated inclusiveness of the egalitarian Qur'anic message, which left the door open for jurists to negotiate some types of abortion as permissible.

82. Hick, *Evil and the God of Love*, 13.

83. William L. Rowe, "The Problem of Evil and Some Varieties of Atheism," in *The Evidential Argument from Evil*, ed. Daniel Howard-Snyder (Bloomington, IN: Indiana University Press, 1996), 4.

84. Hick, *Evil and the God of Love*, 314.

85. Sarra Tlili, *Animals in the Qur'an* (New York: Cambridge University Press, 2012), 206.

86. al-Faḍl b. al-Ḥasan al-Ṭabarsī, *Majmaʿ al-bayān* (Beirut: Dār al-Murtaḍā, 2006),7:270.

87. Tlili, *Animals in the Qur'an*, 207–208.

88. Ibid., 206.

89. As in, for example, Q. 14:13, 17:39, 53:10.

90. I prefer translating *awḥā* as "reveal" over "inspire," as the latter word better serves as an equivalent for the verb *alhama*.

91. Abū ʿAbd Allāh Muḥyī al-Din Ibn ʿArabī, *al-Juzʾ al-awwal [al-thānī] min Tafsīr al-Shaykh al-Akbar al-ʿārif bi-Llāh Muḥyī al-Dīn Ibn ʿArabī* (Cairo: Muṣṭafā al-Bābī al-Ḥalabī, 1900), 207.

92. Muḥammad b. ʿUzayr al-Sijistānī, *Kitāb Gharīb al-Qurʾān al-musammā bi-Nuzhat al-qulūb* (Cairo: Maṭbaʿat al-Saʿāda, 1907), 249.

93. Malise Ruthven, *Islam in the World* (Oxford: Oxford University Press, 2006), 105.

94. Fāḍil al-Sāmarāʾī, *ʿAlā ṭarīq al-tafsīr al-bayānī* (Sharjah: Jāmiʿat al-Shāriqa Markaz al-Buḥūth wa-l-Darasāt al-Shāriqa, 2005), 2:255.

95. Rumi, *Signs of the Unseen*, 81.

96. Roger Allen, *An Introduction to Arabic Literature* (Cambridge: Cambridge University Press, 2005), 39.

97. Riḍā, *Tafsīr al-manār*, 7:397.

98. Abū Ḥāmid al-Ghazālī, *al-Iqtiṣād fī l-Iʿtiqād*, with commentary and notes by Inṣāf Ramaḍān (Damascus and Beirut: Dār Qutayba, 2003), 126.

99. Rowe, "The Problem of Evil," 5.

100. Ibn ʿĀshūr, *al-Taḥrīr wa-l-tanwīr*, 30:143.

101. Ibn ʿAbbās, *Tanwīr al-miqbās*, 637.

102. Ibid.

103. This view is supported by some hadiths as well. According to this view, animals are judged and even punished in the hereafter for wronging each other. I dismiss this view for not having any Qur'anic textual support and limit myself to my Qur'anic-based research methodology and to what the Qur'an asserts.

104. al-Qurṭubī, *al-Jāmiʿ li-aḥkām al-Qurʾān*, 22:97.

105. al-Zamakhsharī, *al-Kashshāf*, 1182.

106. al-Rāzī, *al-Tafsīr al-kabīr*, 31:68.

107. al-Andalusī, *al-Fiṣal*, 1:74.

108. See Q. 2:203, 3:12, 3:158, 4:172, 5:96, 6:51, 6:22, 6:72, 6:128, 6:111, 8:24, 8:36, 10:28, 10:45, 15:25, 7:97, 18:47, 19:68, 19:85, 20:59, 20:102, 20:124–25, 23:79, 25:17, 25:34, 27:17, 27:83, 34:40, 37:22, 41:19, 46:6, 50:44, 59:2, 58:9, 67:24, 79:25.

109. al-Rāzī, *al-Tafsīr al-kabīr*, 12:222.

110. Ibid., 229.

111. Bernstein, *Radical Evil*, 227.

112. Nagīb Maḥfūẓ, *al-Liṣṣ wa-l-kilāb* (Cairo: Dār Miṣr, 1961).

113. Richard E. Singer, *Job's Encounter* (New York: Bookman Associates, 1963), 210.

114. Voltaire, *Candide*, with an introduction by Philip Littell (New York: The Modern Library, 1918), 17.

115. Singer, *Job's Encounter*, 210.

116. Jean-Paul Sartre, *Existentialism and Human Emotions* (New York: Philosophical Library, 1957), 16.

# *Chapter 4*

# Rethinking the End of the Journey

## *Reevaluating Islamic Apocalyptic Literature*

I began the book by arguing against the illusion that the start of our worldly journey was a punishment. In this chapter, I discuss another illusion, namely, a guaranteed worldly happy ending that humankind is entitled to. In the lives of nations, like in the lives of individuals, happy endings are not guaranteed. The end—at least from a Qur'anic view—does not lie here. However, according to a widespread line of traditional apocalyptic thinking, the end of the world is preceded by a radical and final cosmic resolution of the problem of evil. In this chapter, I discuss core elements of this literature and compare them to what is confirmed in the Qur'an. As a conclusion of my argument, I reject many aspects of the traditional Islamic apocalyptic narrative for three reasons: first, because it merely reflects a human yearning for closure that escapes human individual responsibility; second, because it lacks any Qur'anic textual support; and third, because it contradicts core concepts of the Qur'anic assessment of the problem of evil.

As I explain, variable apocalyptic narratives promoting the concept of an awaited savior have been conceptualized cross-religiously and cross-culturally to serve the same purpose as the collective sense of responsibility, one that is subconsciously suppressed by shifting the responsibility of ending all worldly evil to a future figure. While this figure—who usually never comes!—holds the sole responsibility of miraculously bringing about all desired happy endings, including bringing the problem of evil itself to an end, the rest have no responsibility of changing or doing anything to facilitate or accelerate his arrival! To the contrary, all what the believing people have to do is to wait patiently and never lose their faith in the savior's coming.

## ISLAMIC APOCALYPTIC LITERATURE AND THE HUMAN YEARNING FOR CLOSURE

As I explain in detail, multifaceted religious and mythological beliefs advocate for future eschatological saviors and fantasize about an ultimate human happiness, conditional on their appearance. Islamic apocalyptic literature describes a series of events that will eventually lead to the final annihilation of the world. These events include the second coming of Jesus, who will fight the Islamic version of the Antichrist, or al-Masīḥ al-Dajjāl. He will miraculously defeat him thereby bringing to an end an era of chaos, turmoil, and mass corruption. In addition, despite substantial variations in the related details, for the Shia and Sunnis alike, the Mahdi, who will appear toward the end of time to restore justice to the world, comes also to echo this yearning for a missing worldly justice and to confirm the rationale of waiting for a savior.

Before we delve into my objections to the traditional Islamic version of the end-of-time narrative provided by exegetical literature, a quick survey of the image as it is portrayed in some other religions can unearth interesting similarities. Easily observable syncretism manifests itself in many mythological and religious apocalypses that share similar visions of a radical worldly defeat of evil. In addition, they all share nourishing a troublesome human tendency to shift the individual responsibility to combat evil to others: a human sacrifice, a redeemer, or to an awaited savior or eschatological figure who can bring the pain and suffering of others to an end.

Ideologies promoting avoiding responsibility, shifting responsibility to others, and even waiting for a savior who can magically change all what needs to be changed are found almost everywhere, in the lives of individuals and in the lives of peoples and nations. Most notably, these ideas found their way to religions themselves. As a result, beliefs advocating for passive submission and helpless waiting replace the more progressive and more active values that allowed those religions to be conceptualized as social and political phenomena in the first place. A look at similarities embodied in cross-cultural religious thinking can reveal a shared tendency to escape individual responsibility. In many ancient religious traditions, the idea of a human sacrifice or even an animal offering for deities came to idolize the desire that salvific suffering of some can exempt the rest from pain and can guarantee them unconditional prosperity and divine blessings. Suffering is enormously terrifying as a collective destiny; therefore, all means of maximizing the suffering of some chosen victims were pursued across those practices as an essential requirement for others to set themselves free from it. For example, the suffering and tears of children the Aztecs priests used to choose as human sacrifices for the rain god Tlaloc, the anguish of their parents who had to give up the lives of their children, and even the suffering of the crowds that watched them paraded before their final slaughter were all thought of as essential rituals to "augur rain."[1] In Judaism, the Messiah is usually conceived of as "the perfect realization of the character of the theocratic king."[2] In the Messiah, "the heart's yearning would find absolute satisfaction. His coming was the goal of Hope; in it would be found the final fulfillment of all that had been promised to the fathers. Each successive prophet only pointed to Him; each righteous and successful king only typified Him; but men did not dream of looking beyond Him and His times."[3] In Christianity, this line of messianic thinking is crystallized in two ways: first, in thinking of Jesus as the political leader who will return at the end of time to defeat the Antichrist and establish the kingdom of God here on earth; and second, in thinking of him as the savior and the redeemer who can use his own suffering—which was like the ancient human sacrifices maximized in all possible ways—as a way to prevent all his followers from suffering. In Zoroastrianism, a legend of three future saviors—who will be born of Zoroaster seed after his death—which "is only fully developed in Pahlavi literature"[4] seems to be echoing the same desire. As Carlo comments, "Scholars have endeavored to elucidate parallels to the Zoroastrian eschatological narration in other traditions, and have sometimes been able to spot convincing correspondences for individual passages and themes, but not for the narration as a whole."[5] Similarly, Maitreya in Buddhism is thought of as the future Buddha. Alan Sponberg elaborates on the variety seen in the cultural adoption of this "appealing figure":[6]

> The story of Maitreya, the future Buddha, became a tradition that has played some role, often a central one, in the cultural history of virtually every period and every area of Buddhist Asia. Indeed, one finds a variety of quite distinctive expressions of that tradition, a variety that often obscures the underlying motifs that have tended to persist throughout Maitreya's variegated development and transformation. The Maitreya legend has provided a symbol rich in possibility for culturally specific, local elaboration, yet it has also continued throughout to draw on a group of core themes and—aspirations deeply rooted in the Buddhist culture common to most of Asia. Every Buddhist culture has appropriated this appealing figure, each in its own way, and it is because of this historical development of cultural variations on a set of common themes that a study of Maitreya's many guises provides a superb opportunity to observe the fascinating process by which Buddhism shaped, and was shaped by, a series of cultural encounters reaching across Asia from the Deccan to the islands of Japan.[7]

I recognize this overview of very complex traditions is reductive and cursory, and that many scholars have addressed important nuances in specialized writing. My only purpose here is to emphasize just how common this tendency to escape individual responsibility is. What matters most is the easily observed tendency in all these accounts to first, fantasize about solutions devoid of individual responsibility, which instead place the onus of bringing about the desired changes to "the awaited other," whoever that other might be; and second, promote an illusion of a perfect and ideal ending of all worldly evil. For example, the glorious time after the second coming of Jesus, as Ibn Kathīr describes,[8] is envisioned as a time of ultimate abundance, harmony, and peace. It is a time when children will play safely with snakes and when lions and camels, cows and tigers, sheep and wolves, will all live peacefully together! Also, interestingly enough, all the previous accounts seem to be responding to the problem of evil in a similar way by suggesting eras of uncontrollable global evil, bloodshed, greed, and immorality that will necessarily precede the miraculous appearance of those figures. As Joseph M. Kitagawa (1915–1992) rightly notes,

> Clearly, the notion that the future promises to be better than the present, leading to the triumph of the good at the end of the world, is based not on empirical observation, but on speculation and affirmation. Such speculation and affirmation are often associated with a religious vision of the coming of the cosmic ruler, universal king, or world savior at the end, as we find in various religious traditions, East and West. There are as well negative forms of progressivism, which view the future in terms of a successive erosion of values, though this is still often associated with a belief in the coming of a supramundane figure who redresses all evils at the end of the world.[9]

It strikes one as very odd that all these solutions variably but equally propose solutions capable of correcting mistakes, bringing about world justice, and even forgiveness and salvation in the afterlife via eschatological figures with minimum effort required by the adherents themselves. In one way or another, the idea of "a supernatural being, who at the end of time would bring back Order and Justice which had been banished from the world, and thus prelude the Kingdom of immortality and endless bliss"[10] is similarly implemented to indicate the all-too-human psychological desire to escape responsibility.

In Islamic traditional literature, the same account of the second coming of Jesus and his final battle with al-Masīḥ al-Dajjāl (the charlatan Messiah) was successfully implemented to ensure a responsibility-free narrative of a worldly happy ending—one that the Qur'an never promised. Adopting the story, though, needed some modifications that theologians were ready to provide as influenced by Biblical narratives. Eventually they ended up with a new hybrid story that narrates the same Christian story after adding to it an Islamic flavor. Jesus, according to the Islamic version of the story, will come back to break the cross and to endorse Islam and not Christianity as the sound religion. Second, because the second element was missing from the picture, that is, Jesus as a redeemer, Muhammad—instead of Jesus—was this time portrayed as filling this role. Again, in a similar attempt to escape responsibility and despite the lack of any textual support from the Qur'an or the many counter assurances of personal responsibility, Muhammad was portrayed as the provider of *shafāʿa* (intercession), which will enable some wrongdoers and sinners among his followers redemption.[11] Finally, the Mahdi was introduced to set the stage for a complete Islamic salvific scenario, one that can be equally applied to the worldly life and hereafter. While many still adopt this narrative, some like Rashīd Riḍā soundly criticize the way Muslims portray the Mahdi as the leader who brings them back their glorious days and removes all worldly injustice by working miracles.[12]

## ISLAMIC APOCALYPTIC LITERATURE AND THE LACK OF QUR'ANIC TEXTUAL SUPPORT

Riḍā criticized such line of apocalyptic wishful thinking in Islam and labeled it as harmful.[13] Contrary to the above widely circulated beliefs, like the belief in Muhammad as a redeemer, the Qur'an came, as Muḥammad Farīd Wajdī (1878–1954) argues,[14] to dispel this line of wishful thinking as it is made clear in, "It will not be according to your hopes or those of the People of the Book: anyone who does wrong will be required for it and will find no one to protect or help him against God" (4:123). As Muṣṭafā Maḥmūd makes clear, this suspect endorsement of the doctrine of *shafāʿa* served only to provide Muslims with a hard choice between "the Qur'anic negation of it and what was asserted in Sunna."[15]

Regardless of the temporary relief these narratives provide, they can do much harm than good in the long run, not to mention the shortcomings of their deceptive and illusory nature. The Qur'anic text doesn't provide any support for the traditional apocalyptic narratives. The second coming of Jesus is not mentioned in the Qur'an and "there is no text in the Qur'an which proves that Jesus will descend from the heavens to rule on earth."[16] Even exegetes who supported apocalyptic narratives had to appeal to hadith or to interpretive tactics to justify their *tafsīr*, like al-Shaʿrāwī, for example, who had to apply the following verse, "We have sent down the message to you too [Prophet], so that you can explain[17] to people what was sent for them, so that they may reflect" (16:44) to his interpretation of "God said, 'Jesus, I will take you back and raise you up to Me: I will purify you of the disbelievers" (3:55) to support his argument for the second coming of Jesus.[18] Al-Shaʿrāwī had to indirectly infer the credibility and the authenticity of his claim by way of juxtaposing the role of the Prophet as an interpreter of the Qur'an, which is a Qur'anic claim, and the assertion of the second advent of Jesus, which is a non-Qur'anic claim and can be found only in hadith. Also, it is important to remember that while some verses were metaphorically interpreted by some exegetes as referring to Jesus and his second coming, there is no single mention of al-Masīḥ al-Dajjāl or the Mahdi that can be located in the Qur'anic text! In al-Bukhārī's hadith collection, considered by many as the most authentic, al-Masīḥ al-Dajjāl is described as a bone-chilling, evil, one-eyed figure,[19] who will appear toward the end of time. He will be given miracles and signs that will lead many people astray as he travels throughout the globe.[20]

The lack of credibility of the apocalyptic literature in Islam is based on an exegetical flaw I refer to as "the use of hadith to invalidate the Qur'anic text."[21] The Qur'anic narrative asserts very few facts about the life of Jesus. Jesus, according to the Qur'an, was saved from crucifixion as we read,

> And so for breaking their pledge, for rejecting God's revelations, for unjustly killing their prophets, for saying "Our minds are closed"—No! God has sealed them in their disbelief, so they believe only a little—and because they disbelieved and uttered a terrible slander against Mary, and said, "We have killed the Messiah, Jesus, son of Mary, the Messenger of God." (They did not kill him, nor did they crucify him, though it was made to appear like that to them; those that disagreed about him are full of doubt, with no knowledge to follow, only supposition: they certainly did not kill him—No! God raised him up to Himself. God is almighty and wise. (4:155–58)

As Riḍā points out, Judas Iscariot according to the Gospels' narratives had to identify Jesus for arrest by kissing him, which assures that "soldiers didn't know Jesus in person."[22] He refers also to a confusion among exegetes who, in their majority, followed what they were told by the converts among Jews and Christian scholars who were divided themselves in their views.[23] As he asserts, Muslims unanimously believe that Jesus was saved from those who confused him with another person, who was killed instead of Jesus.[24] The second coming of Jesus is not asserted anywhere in the Qur'an. The majority of exegetical attempts made to justify such a belief are based on interpretive choices that prioritized a metaphorical and figurative approach to the literal one. For example, a verse that exegetes "changed its meaning to fit narratives indicating the physical ascension of the body of Jesus to the heavens"[25] is found in chapter 3, " God said, 'Jesus, I will take you back and raise you up to Me: I will purify you of the disbelievers'" (3:55). While the majority of exegetes argued for this verse as indicating a physical as well as a spiritual ascension that includes both the body and the soul of Jesus, Riḍā followed his teacher, Muḥammad ʿAbduh, in arguing for "taking Jesus" as a reference to his "normal death,"[26] which was followed by the ascension of his soul. More importantly, Riḍā refers to the belief in the ascension and the second coming of Jesus as Christian doctrines that found their way to Islam through Jewish convert exegetes like Wahb ibn Munabbih and Ka'b al-Aḥbār.[27] Al-Sha'rāwī asserts the moot nature of this verse and leaves it open to a variety of interpretations, because one's faith doesn't depend on the way one might understand or interpret this verse.[28]

## ISLAMIC APOCALYPTIC LITERATURE AND THE CONTRADICTION WITH THE QUR'ANIC ASSESSMENT OF THE PROBLEM OF EVIL

As Brockopp soundly observes, "Although Islamic rituals emphasize the importance of community, Islamic theology promotes individual, not communal, salvation."[29] The Qur'an when read in isolation from the later developed Islamic literature and hadith—which as we have seen are full of a vivid apocalyptic content—and from a long history of exegetical modification, which reshaped most of its content, never asserts an escape or refuge from human individual responsibility. While I remain strictly Qur'anic in my research methodology in this book and avoid dealing with the detailed traditional apocalyptic narratives, I refer to general deep contradictions[30] between the Qur'anic-announced conceptualization of the end of time and the Qur'anic assessment of the problem of evil, on one hand, and the exegetical reconstructed image, on the other. It is very important to remember that not only do we not have any textual support of the traditional apocalyptic narrative, but in addition, the analytical reading of the Qur'anic text falsifies the credibility of the exegetical view for the following thorny reasons.

First, the traditional image assumes a monolithic religious reality as the ending scene in the history of our human religiosity. It views religious pluralism as negative, contrary to what we see in the Qur'an. According to the traditional narrative "Christ's return is part of Allah's larger plan of bringing the world under the rule of Islam."[31]

Jesus will descend at the end of time to "end the *jizya* taxation, break the cross and kill al-Masīḥ al-Dajjāl."[32] More importantly, Jesus will curtail Christianity and Judaism and accept nothing but Islam as the only sound religion.[33] All his contemporary Christians and Jews (*ahl al-kitāb*) will follow him in converting to Islam. This picture of the domination of one religion is very problematic, though. First, because it violates religious pluralism as a well-rooted and divinely intended Qur'anic principle as we read in, "If your Lord had pleased, He would have made all people a single community, but they continue to have their differences" (11:118). The full affirmation of religious pluralism in the Qur'an can be found in many places like in," The

[Muslim] believers, the Jews, the Christians, and the Sabians—all those who believe in God and the Last Day and do good—will have their rewards with their Lord. No fear for them, nor will they grieve" (2:62). Second, because it contradicts the way the Qur'an predicts the history of human experience of religion as it departs from asserting religious pluralism as a norm that continues as long as humans occupy earth. As the Qur'an literally confirms, religious disputes and conflicts will be resolved only on the Day of Judgment and only with help from divine intervention, "As for the believers, those who follow the Jewish faith, the Sabians, the Christians, the Magians, and the idolaters, God will judge between them on the Day of Resurrection" (22:17). Third, this interpretation portrays for no good reason Muhammad's mission as an unfinished project. Instead, it provides Jesus the legitimacy of ending a project that Muhammad did not himself authorize or advocate for. That is, the so-called need for the radical annihilation and cancellation of previous revelations. Contrary to this unfair image, "Islam considered itself from the beginning a continuum, not a negation, of other heavenly religions."[34] Islam, as Muhammad preached, was not an abrogation of the previous monotheistic traditions but a reactivation and a purification thereof. The Qur'an came as a confirmation of the previous traditions as we read in, "Children of Israel, remember how I blessed you, Honour your pledge to Me and I will honour My pledge to you: I am the One you should fear. Believe in the message I have sent down confirming what you already possess. Do not be the first to reject it, and do not sell My messages for a small price: be mindful of Me" (2:40–41). More importantly, the Islamic legislation, as the Qur'an confirms, was completed and perfected with Muhammad as we read in, "Today I have perfected your religion for you" (5:3). Therefore, the eradication of Christianity and Judaism that Jesus will allegedly bring about in his putative second coming is not an Islamic project per se because first, it does not fit but contradicts the mission of Islam; and second, it portrays Islam as an unfinished project contrary to the previously mentioned Qur'anic confirmation.

Second, the traditional apocalyptic account contradicts the Qur'anic account of the Day of Judgment. First, the traditional account echoes the previously explained human yearning for an earthly closure and assumes an earthly happy ending that renders the Day of Judgment superfluous. Our story as humans on earth does start but does not end here. Therefore, any theological or spiritual approach that tries to make sense of life's injustices and contradictions remains inconsistent without the belief in an afterlife justice. It is the reason why the belief in the Day of Judgment and the hereafter is mentioned in the Qur'an as an essential criterion for salvation. Interestingly enough, the Qur'anic tripartite of salvation doesn't pinpoint one religion in a clear assertion of its broad monotheistic message, but asserts instead the following three dimensions as essential for the soundness of the faith adopted by believers:

(1) belief in one God, (2) belief in the Day of Judgment, and (3) a commitment to righteous deeds, which can practically echo the first two beliefs, "The [Muslim] believers, the Jews, the Christians, and the Sabians—all those who believe in God and the Last Day and do good—will have their rewards with their Lord. No fear for them, nor will they grieve" (2:62). God is described in the Qur'an as the judge of the Day of Resurrection, who will eventually put all world injustices, contested disputes, and conflicts to an end, "[Prophet], it is your Lord who will judge between them on the Day of Resurrection concerning their differences" (32:25), Second, the Day of Resurrection, as the Qur'an confirms, comes suddenly, contrary to the exacerbating plan of events vividly described in Islamic apocalyptic literature, "They ask you [Prophet] about the Hour, 'When will it arrive?' Say, 'My Lord alone has knowledge of it: He alone will reveal when its time will come, a time that is momentous in both the heavens and earth. All too suddenly it will come upon you'" (7:187). Riḍā alluded in his criticism of the hadith-based traditional belief in al-Masīḥ al-Dajjāl to this contradiction and labeled it as "problematic."[35]

Third, the traditional apocalyptic narrative claims access to the unseen, which is preserved in the Qur'an as a divine right. Details of events preceding the final perdition and destruction of the world as we know it, which are normally ascribed to the Prophet, indicate access to foreknowledge that contradicts what the Qur'an affirms. Foreknowledge, as the Qur'an asserts, is a divine faculty: "He has the keys to the unseen: no one knows them but Him" (6:59). The Prophet, as the Qur'an affirms literally, denies any claim to the unseen as we read in, "Say [Prophet], 'I have no control over benefit or harm, [even] to myself, except as God may please: if I had knowledge of what is hidden, I would have abundant good things and no harm could touch me. I am no more than a bearer of warning, and good news to those who believe'" (7:188). In addition, as the Qur'an confirms, informing about the unseen when exceptionally provided to the Prophet happens via revelation. Now, understanding the Qur'an as heavenly revelation which the Prophet received from God means that apocalyptic visions should be textually supported; otherwise, how can they be justified? In other words, had the Prophet received apocalyptic visions these visions should have been Qur'anic verses. The Prophet, as the Qur'an describes above, has no access to the unseen, which goes beyond his knowledge. Therefore, other than what is textually revealed to him, the Prophet cannot confirm or deny anything. This includes what took place in the past: "This account is part of what was beyond your knowledge [Muhammad]. We revealed it to you: you were not present with Joseph's brothers when they made their treacherous plans" (12:102), and includes what might take place in the future: "They ask you [Prophet] about the Hour, 'When will it arrive?' Say, 'My Lord alone has knowledge of it: He alone will reveal when its time will come, a time that is momentous in both the heavens and earth'" (7:187).

Fourth, the inconsistency of the hadith-based apocalyptic literature. The Islamic consensus on the soundness of hadiths of al-Masīḥ al-Dajjāl,[36] the affirmation of many scholars of the historical acceptance made by cleric and Imams of those hadiths,[37] and the claim that "it is not permissible for any Muslim to doubt or deny them"[38]—leave behind questions concerning the many internal contradictions and discrepancies in apocalyptic hadith narratives, which should have led, as Riḍā argues, to their dismissal.[39] The same concern applies to hadiths of the Mahdi. As Riḍā explains,[40] contradictions in hadiths of the Mahdi are even stronger and more clear, which makes the reconciliation between different narratives harder. This is the reason, he argues, that the two sound collections of hadith (of al-Bukhārī and Muslim, respectively) do not include any of the Mahdi hadiths. This concern does not deal with the contradiction between hadith and Qur'an, or the many concerns surrounding the credibility of preserved hadith collections, but addresses hadith collections themselves, which fail to provide a coherent apocalyptic narrative.[41] In the following I refer only to some examples to provoke rethinking the traditional consensus without dealing with concrete contradictions from specific hadiths for exceeding the pure Qur'anic methodology I adopt in this book. For example, the progress of human history is portrayed as unfolding a degradation in morality according to one sound hadith.[42] The same line of argument affirms that the end of time will be witnessed by the most evil people,[43] in an era when Islam ends up strange the same way it started[44] and when no one says "Allah" anymore.[45] However, this line of argument contradicts another utopian image equally affirmed in sound collections of hadith. According to this image, the end of time is marked by a series of events that end with the descending of Jesus, who will rule the world and restore justice to it in an era of bounty and prosperity.[46] This ideal era will witness the absence and disappearance of all hatred, envy, and jealousy between people.[47]

Another glaring contraction stems from a problematic inconsistency in the chronological order of events Islamic apocalyptic literature provides. Al-Mahdi according to the mainstream narrative will either shortly precede al-Masīḥ al-Dajjāl or be a contemporary of him. According to many narratives al-Mahdi will help Jesus in killing al-Masīḥ al-Dajjāl and will even be asked by al-Masīḥ to lead the Muslims prayer immediately after his ascendance![48] The time of al-Mahdi, which is supposed to last for seven, eight, or a maximum of nine years,[49] as these narratives describe is a time of abundance, prosperity and blessing.[50] However, ironically enough, the time when al-Masīḥ al-Dajjāl appears is described as a time of hardship and severe drought that causes animals to die.[51] The clear contradiction in narratives leaves one puzzled on how to describe the time when the three main figures: al-Masīḥ, al-Mahdi and al-Masīḥ al-Dajjāl will supposedly coexist and whether it is going to be a time of unlimited abundance or a time of an unimaginable famine and hardship! Even the estimation of the seriousness and the danger of al-Masīḥ al-Dajjāl seems to have received conflicting estimations if different narrations are to be equally considered. While some hadiths seem to be belittling the influence of al-Masīḥ al-Dajjāl and his limited powers[52] other hadiths both in the two sound collections of hadith ascribe to him mighty powers and supernatural abilities including the ability of restricting the dead![53]

The list of—equally supported—internal contradictions goes beyond what I am interested in providing a space for here. To mention some though, there are contradictions concerning the nature of al-Masīḥ al-Dajjāl. In the famous Jassasah hadith, which the hadith collection of *Sunan Abi Dawud* includes, Tamim al-Dari, a Christian, who came and accepted Islam, narrates to the Prophet an encounter of a group of men who were lost in a sea storm with al-Masīḥ al-Dajjāl on an isolated island. According to this hadith, al-Masīḥ al-Dajjāl is described as a huge and strong man chained to his knees and who was waiting to be given the permission to emerge.[54] However, in another hadith in the same collection al-Masīḥ al-Dajjāl is described as a short man![55] To all these concerns we should add controversies from the many narratives concerning the mysterious figure known as Ibn Sayyad, allegedly a Jew who lived in Medina and converted to Islam, and the so-called insistence of some of the companions on identifying him as al-Masīḥ al-Dajjāl!

With these few examples I leave behind this external research which doesn't fit my Qur'anic methodology and satisfy by leaving this concern as an underdeveloped footnote for those who wholeheartedly take this literature at face value. In short, this chapter provides an invitation to rethink the divinity of our human journey, the responsibility as God's gods on earth, and the Qur'anic assessment of the problem of evil for an elevation of Islamic apocalyptic tradition to what can be truly described as authentically Qur'anic.

## NOTES

1. Inga Clendinnen, *Aztecs: An Interpretation* (Cambridge: Cambridge University Press,1995), 138.
2. Vincent Henry, *The Jewish and the Christian Messiah* (Edinburgh: T. & T. Clark, 1886), 147.
3. Ibid., 147–48.
4. Carlo G. Cereti, "Myths, Legends, Eschatologies," in *The Wiley Blackwell Companion to Zoroastrianism*, ed. Michael Stausberg and Yuhan Sohrab-Dinshaw Vevaina (Chichester, UK: John Wiley & Sons, 2015), 270.
5. Ibid., 271.

6. Alan Sponberg, "Introduction," in *Maitreya: The Future Buddha*, ed. Alan Sponberg and Helen Hardacre (Cambridge: Cambridge University Press, 1988), 2.

7. Ibid.

8. Ibn Kathīr, *Tafsīr al-Qur'ān al-'aẓīm*, 2:457.

9. Joseph M. Kitagawa, "The Many Faces of Maitreya," in *Maitreya*, 8.

10. James Darmesteter, *The Mahdi: Past and Present* (London: T. F. Unwin, 1885), 2.

11. al-Bukhārī, *Ṣaḥīḥ al-Bukhārī*, 1629 (hadith no. 6566); Muslim b. al-Ḥajjāj, *Ṣaḥīḥ Muslim* (Riyadh: Dār Ṭayyiba, 2006), 112 (hadith no. 334/198).

12. Riḍā, *Tafsīr al-manār*, 9:499.

13. Riḍā, *Tafsīr al-manār*, 6:57.

14. Muḥammad Farīd Wajdī, *Muqaddimat ṣafwat al-'irfān fī tafsīr al-Qur'ān* (Cairo: Maṭba'at al-Sha'b, 1903), 174.

15. Muṣṭafā Maḥmūd, *al-Shafā'a* (Cairo: Akhbār al-Yawm, 1999), 11.

16. Riḍā, *Tafsīr al-manār*, 6:59.

17. As it is clear from the context, it is an explanation that takes place through the revealed message which is the Qur'anic message. I am grateful to a note from an anonymous reviewer.

18. al-Sha'rāwī, *Tafsīr al-Sha'rāwī*, 1505.

19. al-Bukhārī, *Ṣaḥīḥ al-Bukhārī*, 92 (hadith no. 7127).

20. Ibid., 92–93 (hadith no. 7132).

21. Hasan, *Decoding the Egalitarianism of the Qur'an*, 8.

22. Riḍā, *Tafsīr al-manār*, 6:19.

23. Ibid., 20.

24. Ibid.

25. Ibid., 3:316.

26. Ibid., 317.

27. Rashīd Riḍā, *Fatāwā al-Imām Muḥammad Rashīd Riḍā*, ed. Ṣalāḥ al-Dīn al-Munjid and Yūsuf Q. Khūrī (Beirut: Dār al-Kitāb al-Jadīd, 2005), 2025 (fatwa no. 727).

28. al-Sha'rāwī, *Tafsīr al-Sha'rāwī*, 1502.

29. Jonathan E. Brockopp, "Islam and Bioethics: Beyond Abortion and Euthanasia," *Journal of Religious Ethics* 36 (2008): 6.

30. Because I limit myself to the Qur'an, I exclude dealing with the many self-contradictions and internal discrepancies that can be easily found in the Islamic apocalyptic literature.

31. Ross Moret, "Potential for Apocalypse, Violence and Eschatology in the Israel-Palestine Conflict," *Journal of Religion & Society* 10 (2008): 2.

32. Riḍā, *Tafsīr al-manār*, 6:57.

33. Muḥammad al-Ḥanbalī, *al-Buḥūr al-zākhira fī 'ulūm al-ākhira* (Kuwait: Gharās, 2007), 1:513.

34. Burhān Ghaliyūn, *Naqd al-siyāsa al-dawla wa-l-dīn*, 4th ed. (Beirut: al-Markaz al-Thaqāfī al-'Arabī, 2007), 44.

35. Riḍā, *Tafsīr al-manār*, 9:489.

36. Mashārī Sa'īd al-Maṭrafī, *Ārā' Muḥammad Rashīd Riḍā al-'aqā'idiyya* (Kuwait: Maktab al-Imām al-Dhahabī, 2014), 228.

37. Shafīq b. ʿAbd b. ʿAbd Allāh Shuqayr, *Mawqif al-madrasa al-ʿaqliyya al-ḥadītha min al-ḥadīth al-nabawī al-sharīf* (Beirut: al-Maktab al-Islāmī, 1998), 306.

38. Muḥammad Muḥammad Abū Shuhba, *Difāʿ ʿan al-sunna wa-radd shubhat al-mustashriqīn wa-l-kitāb al-muʿāṣirīn* (Cairo: Maṭbaʿat al-Muṣḥaf al-Sharīf, 1961), 217.

39. Riḍā, *Tafsīr al-manār*, 9:490.

40. Ibid., 499.

41. I refer only to a general contradiction, without dealing with concrete contradictions from specific hadiths, so as not to exceed the pure Qur'anic methodology I adopt in this book.

42. al-Bukhārī, *Ṣaḥīḥ al-Bukhārī*, 1750 (hadith no. 7068).

43. al-Bukhārī, *Ṣaḥīḥ al-Bukhārī*, 1750 (hadith no. 7067).

44. Muslim, *Ṣaḥīḥ Muslim*, 77 (hadith no. 232/145).

45. Ibid., 78 (hadith no. 234/148).

46. Ibid., 80 (hadith no. 242/155).

47. Ibid., 81 (hadith no. 243).

48. al-Tawayjarī, Ḥammūd b. ʿAbd Allāh. *Itḥāf al-jamāʿa bi-mā jāʾa fī l-fitan wa-l-malāḥim wa-ashrāṭ al-sāʿa*. Vol. 2. 2nd ed.) Riyadh: Dār al-Ṣamīʿī, 1993), 290–291.

49. Ibid., 279.

50. Ibid., 297.

51. Ibid., 371.

52. al-Bukhārī, Ṣaḥīḥ al-Bukhārī (Damascus: Dār Ibn Kathīr, 2002), 1716, hadith number 7122. Some narratives mentioned reading 10 or even 3 verses of chapter 18 as sufficient to secure protection from al-Masīḥ al-Dajjāl.

53. al-Bukhārī, Ṣaḥīḥ al-Bukhārī (Damascus: Dār Ibn Kathīr, 2002), 1763, hadith number 7132.

54. al-Sijistānī, Abū Dāwūd. Sunan Abī Dāwūd. Vol. 2. Edited by Muḥammad ʿAbd al-ʿAzīz al-Khālidī (Beirut: Dār al-Kutub al-ʿIlmiyya, 1996), 122, hadith numbers 4326 and 4325.

55. Ibid. 120, hadith number 4320.

# Conclusion

The strict Qur'anic methodology I adopt in this book provides an opportunity to examine some core elements concerning the beginning, the end, and even the meaning of our human journey on earth, outside of a long history of exegetical reshaping of what the Qur'anic message confirms. Interestingly enough, the Qur'an itself in one scene that depicts the Day of Judgment is described by the Prophet as an abandoned book (25:30). This prophetic complaint contradicts the everyday experience of all Muslims around the world of the Qur'an as a widely accessible book. The rarely considered acute Qur'anic accusation made by the Prophet himself should motivate us to rethink the real meaning of this abandonment of the Qur'an.

How can one best understand and appreciate this perplexing Qur'anic scene? The Qur'an, as it can be easily observed, accompanies Muslims' lives, daily routines, religious rituals, funerals, weddings, birth sermons, Eid festivals, and so on. In Muslim communities, Qur'anic words are whispered in the ears of newborn babies so that they are the first thing they hear as they start their worldly journey. Likewise, Qur'anic words accompany funerals, which are seldom planned without Qur'anic recitations. A specific, well-known command is given to read chapter 36 to help both the stricken and their families in their last moments. Traditions recommending Muslims to read the Qur'an at least once during Ramadan and to read at least chapter 18 every Friday are still remarkably observed by Muslims around the world. Facebook and Instagram postings, social media accounts, mosque and house decorations, calligraphy, art, poetry, mystic *dhikr*, and even music and songs; they all variably yet systematically celebrate a Qur'anic-based heritage. International competitions for reading and memorizing the Qur'an are annually organized and generously rewarded. So what does this daunting Qur'anic accusation of the abandonment of the Holy Book stand for? Among so many other things, this abandonment might be indeed a reference to the empty ritualistic recitation that has replaced the active reading, the routinely organized sermonizes who replaced honest worship, imitation which replaced innovation. As Omar M. Ramahi observes, while all Muslims are encouraged to read the Qur'an[1] they are rarely encouraged to actively and independently read it!

> Many Muslim individuals and Muslim organizations are ready and quick to hand out copies of the Mushaf to spread the message of Islam. This would give the indication that Muslims want everyone to read the Mushaf independently and learn Islam from its primary (if not only) source. However, the reality is completely different. Once any individual starts contemplating and inquiring about certain verses, the more learned and seasoned Muslims would direct that individual to the "scholars of Islam" who, the scholars believe, interpreted everything that needs to be interpreted for the "rest of us." So one wonders why there is this unusual enthusiasm to hand out the Mushaf if one needs to go through specific channels or certified clergy to understand it. At one time, the Catholic Church did not allow commoners to possess a copy of the Bible. The argument of the Church then was that the interpretation of the Bible had to be made by the Church's sanctioned clergy. The parallel between the Church then and the Muslim clergy now is striking.[2]

In his eloquent elaboration on the need to move with Islamic scholarship beyond blind imitation Hisham Altalib (b. 1940) says,

> As Muslims, we revere religious scholars, especially classical scholars, but we should not blindly act on their statements without considering our own special circumstances and the different time and place that we live in. We ought to make legal decisions by independent interpretation of the Qur'an and the authentic Sunnah through proper ijtihad in such a way as to bear in mind present-day circumstances and the factors of time and place (as scholars did during other eras).[3]

Yet more seriously, the Qur'anic documentation of its own abandonment may be a reference to a long history of exegetical obfuscation of the real Qur'anic message, both arbitrary and deliberate. On the need to "move from blind faith and emulation to faith informed by fact"[4] John Andrew Morrow says,

> From day one, people lied about the Prophet. They suppressed everything. They twisted his teachings. They even tried to corrupt the Qur'ān as can be seen in some of its interpretations and translations. Those lies, deceptions, and deformations continue to affect Islām in a criminal way to this day.[5]

In this book and in an effort to reactivate the authentic Qur'anic voice and to free the "revolutionary Qur'anic message,"[6] I depend solely on the Qur'an to argue for rethinking the unique divine assignment of humans, as

God's gods on earth. From the beginning, Adam was created from earth to live on earth. Adam didn't start his earthly journey in exile but in a divinely provided dwelling. He and his offspring are tested with evil. However, evil afflicts humans due to their divinity, which needs to be proven and reclaimed, not due to their so-called sinful nature. The two concepts of human divinity and evil—when understood as a test—come wrapped inextricably together. We can either live sleepwalking, totally unaware of our divine status, or otherwise, we can mindfully choose to be conscious of every step we take and every decision we make; however, in both cases we will still be fulfilling an unavoidable mission. Rumi says,

> All people then do God's work, ignorant though they may be of God's purpose and even if they have in mind another purpose entirely. God wishes the world to continue; people occupy themselves with their desires and gratify their lusts with women for their own delectation, but from it come children. In this manner they are doing something for their own pleasure while it is actually for the maintenance of the world. They are therefore serving God, although they have no such intention.[7]

My interpretation of the first garden Adam dwelled in as an earthly garden is more consistent with core elements in the Qur'anic narrative. The story is narrated in the Qur'an, not for the purposes of demonizing humanity but as a lesson for Adam's children to learn from. Like their father before them, Adam's offspring—without exception—will have to deal with Satan's ruthless war waged against them. More importantly, like their father many—if not all his offspring—will occasionally fall for Satan's temptation in one way or another. Therefore, the opportunity to learn how to react when we sin is the real reason the whole story was told. As humans, we will never be immune from sinning. Therefore, God's lesson to Adam and to his offspring was to repent when bad things happen. Occasionally falling for Satan's temptation or even repeated sinning, as the Qur'an assures, is not the end of the story as long as humans keep repenting to God. Contrary to the belief that Adam started his earthly journey in exile, Adam had in fact started his honorable journey in an ideal dwelling, and was provided a training opportunity and a practical lesson on God's unconditional forgiveness.

To better appreciate the Qur'anic story, I argue in this book for a distinction that should be made between two core Qur'anic stories. First, the creation of Adam and Eve and the sole exile of the Devil from paradise. Then a story that is usually misinterpreted as repeating or adding more details to the first story. In this second story, Adam and Eve are dismissed form an earthly garden. It is important, then, not to confuse verses when the exile is solely and exclusively addressed to the Devil—which takes place in paradise—and when the exile is addressed to Adam and Eve—which takes place on earth—because the two different types of exile are referring to two different scenes in two different stories; namely, the story of creation and the first test. It is important also not to overlook meticulous Qur'anic linguistic clues that distinguish between the Devil as Iblīs and the Devil as Shayṭān, which stands for his earthly transformation.

The plea for reclaiming this divine status of humans not only helps correct a vestige of a past misconceptions about the beginning of the human journey, it also helps reevaluate religion as a test, better understand all human religiosity challenges, and finally motivates an abandonment of concomitant misleading apocalyptic narratives prompting a guaranteed happy ending and a pseudo supernatural removal of every and all worldly hardship. These narratives, as this book suggests, have no merit other than satisfying the desperate human psychological need for escaping the divine responsibility, essentially associated with being God's own deputy. Evil does exist, both in the lives of nations and in the lives of individuals as well. Instead of denying the existence of evil or blaming God for allowing too much of it; pain, suffering, and evil are best acknowledged and confronted. Evil can be divided into human evil and divine evil. The first is an outcome of abusing the divine in us by abusing our divinely granted free will. The second is best explained as a divine test. While both kinds of evil provide humans a chance to prove their merit, God cannot be blamed for either.

The human story does start but doesn't end here. For those seeking closure an endorsement of other theological elements is a must for the story to be completed. As I argue in this book, any theological effort to evaluate the problem of evil (both human and divine) in isolation from concepts like God's justice, the Day of Judgment, the resurrection of all living beings (including animals), and so on, is deemed to fail. Cherry-picking while approaching theodicy has proven nothing but its inadequacy. This is easily observed in the fact that while many volumes, panels, talks, and discussions are vehemently devoted to the problem of evil, nevertheless the question is as demanding and urgent as it has ever been. In the lives of nations as well as in the lives of people a more mature approach to the problem of evil, which replaces naïve denial by mature consciousness, can be proven to be more effective. The Qur'an, which can be an inspirational source for believers, refers to many lessons that one can learn from the many stories it includes, described in the Qur'an as "the best of stories" (12:3). Job, as the detailed analysis of his story clarifies (see chapter 3), had eventually to seek refuge in God from toxic and self-destructive questioning of suffering and pain. He was praised as an excellent servant for understanding suffering and pain as a test—not as a punishment.

We suffer because we are divine, not because we deserve to. By going up against evil, which starts by understanding it first, we make our statement as God's gods on earth and reclaim our divinity. There is no exit. There is no refuge from our divine responsibility. No worldly outlet is available. Blaming God for life's uncertainties and injustices does not end them. Waiting for saviors accomplishes nothing other than to hinder the true savior awaiting inside each of us. Anguish, evil, and suffering should bring us closer to God instead of estranging us from Him. The painful facing of evil as life's most chilling reality is the first step to liberating ourselves from its pressure. In Jean-Paul Sartre's (1905–1980) *No Exit*,[8] hell is nothing other than being eternally locked up with regrets, resentful ideas, judgments, and scrutiny. Likewise, for some hell might be nothing other than being locked up with the realization that our human battle with evil is eternal. Evil (both human and divine, or what is called natural) has historically survived and will probably survive all our wishes, resentment, curses, sacrifices, tears, and even our most faithful prayers. However, evil is the ultimate test of our divinity, therefore it will continue as long as there remain human beings who deserve to be given a chance to reclaim their divine status.

The acknowledgment of the existence of evil is not an invitation to surrender to it, though, or to feel helpless when afflicted by pain, sickness, anguish, and suffering. Rather, it is an invitation to be better armed while facing evil, better aware of what allows it in the first place, and what it allows for us in terms of reuniting with our true divinity.

The hermeneutical investigation of the Qur'an I include in this book is an invitation to rethink the beginning, the end, and what is in between. As this book demonstrates, many useful arguments in Islamic heritage that unfortunately have been jettisoned, marginalized, or even falsified can be revisited as an alternative approach to the problem of evil and suffering and for the revival of another understanding of the beginning, the end, and the real meaning of our human journey and our divine merit as God's gods on earth.

## NOTES

1. Dr. Ramahi prefers to use the term *Mushaf* to refer to the Qur'an.
2. Omar M. Ramahi, *Muslim's Greatest Challenge* (Black Palm Books, 2019), 32.
3. Hisham Altalib, *Inviting to Islam: Ethics of Engagement* (© Hisham Altalib 1436 AH/2014 CE), 30. Available online from https://www.hishamaltalib.com/library.
4. John Andrew Morrow, *The Most Controversial Qur'anic Verse* (Lanham, MD: Hamilton Books, 2020), 225.
5. Ibid.

6. Ramazan Kılınç, *Islam and Muslims*, online: YouTube, https://www.youtube.com/watch?v=mjpQEAE5PgQ, Aug 5, 2016.

7. Rumi, *Signs of the Unseen*, 108.

8. Jean-Paul Sartre, *No Exit and Three Other Plays* (New York: Vintage Books, 1955).

# Bibliography


Abdel Haleem, Muhammad A. S. *The Qur'an*. New York: Oxford University Press, 2010.

'Abduh, Muḥammad. *Durūs min al-Qur'ān*. Cairo: Dār al-Hilāl, 1959.

Abū Shuhba, Muḥammad Muḥammad. *Difāʿ ʿan al-sunna wa-radd shubhat al-mustashriqīn wa-l-kitāb al-muʿāṣirīn*. Cairo: Maṭbaʿat al-Muṣḥaf al-Sharīf, 1961.

Abū Zayd, Naṣr Ḥāmid. *al-Naṣṣ al-sulṭa al-ḥaqīqa*. Beirut: al-Markaz al-Thaqāfī al-ʿArabī, 1995.

Abū Zayd, Naṣr Ḥāmid. *al-Tafkīr fī zaman al-takfīr*. Cairo: Maktaba Madbūlī, 1995.

Allen, Roger. *An Introduction to Arabic Literature*. Cambridge: Cambridge University Press, 2005.

Altalib, Hisham. *Inviting to Islam: Ethics of Engagement*. © Hisham Altalib 1436 AH/2014 CE. https://www.hishamaltalib.com/library.

Amīr, Jābir b. Idrīs b. ʿAlī. *Maqālat al-tashbīh wa-mawqif ahl al-sunna minhā*. Cairo: Dār Aḍwā' al-Salaf, 2002.

al-Andalusī, Ibn Ḥazm. *al-Fiṣal fī l-milal wa-l-ahwā' wa-l-niḥal*. Cairo: Maktabat al-Salām al-ʿIlmiyya, 1923.

al-ʿAskarī, Abū Hilāl. *al-Furūq al-lughawiyya*. Beirut: Dār al-Kutub al-ʿIlmiyya, 2000.

al-ʿAynī, Badr al-Dīn. *ʿUmdat al-qāri': Sharḥ Ṣaḥīḥ al-Bukhārī*. Beirut: Dār al-Kutub al-ʿIlmiyya, 2001.

Bernstein, Richard. *Radical Evil: A Philosophical Interrogation*. Cambridge, MA: Blackwell Publishers Inc., 2002.

al-Biqāʿī, Burhān al-Dīn. *Naẓm al-durar*. Cairo: Dār al-Kitāb al-Islāmī, 1984.

Birnbaum, David. *God and Evil*. Hoboken, NJ: Ktav Publishing House, 1989.

Bodman, Whitney S. *The Poetics of Iblis: Narrative Theology in the Qur'an*. Cambridge, MA: Harvard University Press, 2011.

Braun, David. "Empty Names, Fictional Names, Mythical Names," *NoÛs* 39 (2005): 596–631.

Brockopp, Jonathan E. "Islam and Bioethics: Beyond Abortion and Euthanasia," *Journal of Religious Ethics* 36 (2008): 3–12.

Brockopp, Jonathan E. "Islam" In *Evil and Suffering*, edited by Jacob Neusner, 120–141. Eugene, OR: Wipf and Stock, 2007.

al-Bukhārī, Muḥammad. *Saḥīḥ al-Bukhārī*. Damascus: Dār Ibn Kathīr, 2002.

Cabrera, Isabel. "Is God Evil?" In *Rethinking Evil*, edited by Maria Pia Lara, 17–26. Berkeley: University of California Press, 2001.

Caplan, Bryan. *The Myth of the Rational Voter*. Princeton, NJ: Princeton University Press, 2007.

Cereti, Carlo G. "Myths, Legends, Eschatologies." In *The Wiley Blackwell Companion to Zoroastrianism*, edited by Michael Stausberg and Yuhan Sohrab-Dinshaw Vevaina, 259–72. Chichester, UK: John Wiley & Sons, 2015.

Chomsky, Noam. *Language and Mind*. Cambridge: Cambridge University Press, 2006.

Clendinnen, Inga. *Aztecs: An Interpretation*. Cambridge: Cambridge University Press, 1995.

Committee of Scholars. *al-Tafsīr al-wasīṭ*. Medina: Maṭbaʿat al-Muṣḥaf al-Sharīf, 1992.

Craig, William Lane. *The Kalām Cosmological Argument*. London: Palgrave Macmillan, 1979.

Darmesteter, James. *The Mahdi: Past and Present*. London: T. F. Unwin, 1885.

Dawkins, Richard. *The God Delusion*. New York: Houghton Mifflin Company, 2006.

Demant, Peter R. *Islam vs. Islamism*. London: Praeger, 2006.

Dews, Peter. *The Idea of Evil*. Malden, MA: Wiley-Blackwell, 2008.

Dostoyevsky, Fyodor. *The Brothers Karamazov*. Translated by Constance Garnett. Grand Rapids, MI: Generic NL Freebook Publisher. http://search.ebscohost.com.libproxy.unl.edu/login.aspx?direct=true&db=nlebk&AN=2009162&site=ehost-live.

Fisher, Mary Pat. *Living Religions*. Boston, MA: Prentice Hall, 2011.

Flescher, Andrew Michael. *Moral Evil*. Washington, DC: Georgetown University Press, 2013.

Ghaliyūn, Burhān. *Naqd al-siyāsa al-dawla wa-l-dīn*. 4th ed. Beirut: al-Markaz al-Thaqāfī al-ʿArabī, 2007.

al-Ghazālī, Abū Ḥāmid. *al-Iqtiṣād fī l-Iʿtiqād*. Commentary and notes by Inṣāf Ramaḍān. Damascus: Dār Qutayba, 2003.

Green, Joey. *Jesus and Muhammad: The Parallel Sayings*. Berkeley, CA: Seastone, 2003.

Green, Peter. *The Problem of Evil*. London: Longmans, Green and Co. 1920.

al-Ḥanbalī, Muḥammad. *al-Buḥūr al-zākhira fī ʿulūm al-ākhira*. Kuwait: Gharās, 2007.

Hasan, Abla. *Decoding the Egalitarianism of the Qur'an: Retrieving Lost Voices on Gender*. Lanham, MD: Lexington Books, 2019.

Hashas, Mohammed, and Mutaz al-Khatib. "Introduction." In *Islamic Ethics and the Trusteeship Paradigm: Taha Abderrahmane's Philosophy in Comparative Perspectives*, edited by Mohammed Hashas and Mutaz al-Khatib, Brill, 2020.

Henry, Vincent. *The Jewish and the Christian Messiah*. Edinburgh: T. & T. Clark, 1886.

Hick, John. *Evil and the God of Love*. London: Macmillan, 1977.

Hoover, Jon. *Ibn Taymiyya's Theodicy of Perpetual Optimism*. Leiden: Brill, 2007.

Hügel, Friedrich. *Essays & Addresses on the Philosophy of Religion*. London: Dent, 1963 [1921].

Hume, David. *Dialogues concerning Natural Religion*. Raleigh, NC: Generic NL Freebook Publisher. http://search.ebscohost.com.libproxy.unl.edu/login.aspx?direct=true&db=nlebk&AN=1085903&site=ehost-live.

Ibn ʿAbbās, ʿAbd Allāh. *Tanwīr al-miqbās min tafsīr Ibn ʿAbbās*. Beirut: Dār al-Kutub al-ʿIlmiyya, 1992.

Ibn ʿArabī, Abū ʿAbd Allāh Muḥyī al-Dīn. *al-Juzʾ al-awwal [al-thānī] min Tafsīr al-Shaykh al-Akbar al-ʿārif bi-Llāh Muḥyī al-Dīn Ibn ʿArabī*. Cairo: Muṣṭafā al-Bābī al-Ḥalabī, 1900.

Ibn ʿArabī, Abū ʿAbd Allāh Muḥyī al-Dīn. *Fuṣūṣ al-ḥikam*. Notes by Abū al-ʿUlā ʿAfīfī. Beirut: Dār al-Kitāb al-ʿArabī, 1946.

Ibn ʿĀshūr, Muḥammad b. al-Ṭāhir. *al-Taḥrīr wa-l-tanwīr*. Tunis: al-Dār al-Tunisiyya, 1984.

Ibn Kathīr, Ismāʿīl b. ʿUmar. *al-Bidāya wa-l-nihāya*. Beirut: Dār al-Maʿārif, 1990.

Ibn Kathīr, Ismāʿīl b. ʿUmar. *Tafsīr al-Qurʾān al-ʿaẓīm*. Riyadh: Dār Ṭayyiba, 1999.

Ibn Qayyim al-Jawziyya, Abū ʿAbd Allāh Muḥammad b. Abī Bakr b. Ayyūb. *Kitāb al-Fawāʾid al-mushawwiq ilā ʿulūm al-Qurʾān wa-ʿilm al-bayān*. Cairo: Maṭbaʿat al-Saʿāda, 1909.

Ibn Qayyim al-Jawziyya, Abū ʿAbd Allāh Muḥammad b. Abī Bakr b. Ayyūb. *Ḥādī al-arwāḥ ilā bilād al-afrāḥ*. Jeddah: Dār ʿĀlam al-Fuʾād, 2007.

Ibn Qutayba, ʿAbd Allāh b. Muslim. *Taʾwil mushkil al-Qurʾān*. Cairo: al-Ḥalabī, 1900.

Ibn Taymiyya, Taqī al-Dīn Aḥmad b. ʿAbd al-Ḥalīm. *al-Risāla al-madaniyya fī taḥqīq al-majāz wa-l-ḥaqīqa fī ṣifāt Allāh Taʿāla*. Riyadh: al-Sunna al-Muḥammadiyya, 2000.

Ibn Taymiyya, Taqī al-Dīn Aḥmad b. ʿAbd al-Ḥalīm. *Majmūʿ al-fatāwā*. Medina: Majmaʿ al-Malik Fahd li-Tibāʿa al-Muṣḥaf al-Sharīf, 2004.

Kant, Immanuel. *Fundamental Principles of the Metaphysics of Morals*. Translated by Thomas Kingsmill Abbott. Raleigh, NC: Generic NL Freebook Publisher. http://search.ebscohost.com.libproxy.unl.edu/login.aspx?direct=true&db=nlebk&AN=1085903&site=ehost-live.

Kellerman, Henry. *The Discovery of God*. New York: Springer, 2013.

al-Kharbūtī, ʿAbd al-Laṭīf. *Tanqīḥ al-kalām fī ʿaqāʾid ahl al-Islām*. Istanbul: Najm Istiqbāl Maṭbaʿasī, 1912.

Kılınç, Ramazan. *Islam and Muslims*, online: YouTube, https://www.youtube.com/watch?v=mjpQEAE5PgQ, Aug 5, 2016.

Kitagawa, Joseph M. "The Many Faces of Maitreya." In *Maitreya: The Future Buddha*, edited by Alan Sponberg and Helen Hardacre, 7–22. Cambridge: Cambridge University Press, 1988.

Larsson, Goran. "The Sound of Satan: Different Aspects of Whispering in Islamic Theology," *Temenos* 48, no.1 (2012): 49–64.

Löfstedt, Torsten. "The Creation and Fall of Adam: A Comparison of the Qur'anic and Biblical Accounts," *Swedish Missiological Themes* 93, no. 4 (2005): 453–477.

Madden, Edward H., and Peter H. Hare. *Evil and the Concept of God*. Springfield, IL: Charles C. Thomas, 1968.

Maḥfūẓ, Nagīb. *al-Liṣṣ wa-l-kilāb*. Cairo: Dār Miṣr, 1961.

Maḥmūd, Muṣṭafā. *al-Shafāʿa*. Cairo: Akhbār al-Yawm, 1999.

Maḥmūd, Muṣṭafā. *Allāh*. Cairo: Akhbār al-Yawm, 2001.

al-Maṭrafī, Mashārī Saʿīd. *Ārāʾ Muḥammad Rashīd Riḍā al-ʿaqāʾidiyya*. Kuwait: Maktab al-Imām al-Dhahabī, 2014.

al-Māturīdī, Abū Manṣūr. *Tāwīlāt al-Qurʾān*. Istanbul: Dār al-Mīzān, 2005.

al-Māwardī, ʿAlī b. Muḥammad. *al-Nukat wa-l-ʿuyūn*. Beirut: Dār al-Kutub al-ʿIlmiyya, 2010.

McAuliffe, Jane Dammen. "Introduction." In *The Cambridge Companion to the Qurʾān*, edited by Jane Dammen McAuliffe, 1–22. Cambridge: Cambridge University Press, 2007.

Mikaberidze, Alexander. *Conflict and Conquest in the Islamic World*. Santa Barbara, CA: ABC-CLIO, 2011.

Moad, Edward Omar. "It's Okay Not to Know God's Plan." Yaqeen Institute, November 5, 2020, accessed 4/17/2021, https://yaqeeninstitute.org/edward-omar-moad/its-okay-not-to-know-gods-plan

Moret, Ross. "Potential for Apocalypse, Violence and Eschatology in the Israel-Palestine Conflict," *Journal of Religion & Society* 10 (2008): 1–14.

Morrow, John Andrew. *The Most Controversial Qurʾanic Verse*. Lanham, MD: Hamilton Books, 2020.

Muslim b. al-Ḥajjāj. *Ṣaḥīḥ Muslim*. Riyadh: Dār Ṭayyiba, 2006.

Naʿnāʿa, Ramzī. *al-Isrāʾīliyyāt wa-atharuhā fī kutub al-tafsir*. Damascus: Dār al-Qalam; Beirut: Dār al-Ḍiyāʾ, 1970.

Nietzsche, Friedrich. *Beyond Good and Evil: Prelude to a Philosophy of the Future*. Translated by Marion Faber. New York: Oxford University Press, 1998.

Ormsby, L. Eric. *Theodicy in Islamic Thought: The Dispute over al-Ghazālī's "Best of All Possible Worlds."* Princeton, NJ: Princeton University Press, 1984.

Ozkan, Tubanur Yesilhark. *A Muslim Response to Evil: Said Nursi on the Theodicy: Contemporary Thought in the Islamic World*. New York: Routledge, 2016.

Ozturk, Mustafa. "The Tragic Story of Iblis (Satan) in the Qur'an," *Journal of Islamic Research* 2, no 2 (December 2009): 128–144.

Pihlström, Sami. *Pragmatic Pluralism and the Problem of God*. New York: Fordham University Press, 2013.

al-Qummī, ʿAlī b. Ibrāhīm. *Tafsīr ʿAlī ibn Ibrāhīm*. Qom: Muʾassasat al-Imām al-Mahdī, 2014.

al-Qurṭubī, Muḥammad b. Aḥmad. *al-Jāmiʿ li-aḥkām al-Qurʾān*. Beirut: al-Risāla, 2006.

Ramahi, Omar. *Muslim's Greatest Challenge*. Black Palm Books, 2019.

al-Rāzī, Fakhr al-Dīn Muḥammad b. ʿUmar. *al-Tafsīr al-kabīr*. Beirut: Dār al-Fikr, 1981.

Reynolds, Gabriel Said. "Biblical Background." In *The Wiley Blackwell Companion to the Qur'an*, edited by Andrew Rippin and Jawid Mojaddedi, 61–81. Chichester, UK: Wiley-Blackwell, 2017.

Riḍā, Rashīd. *Tafsīr al-manār*. Egypt: Dār al-Manār, 1947.

Riḍā, Rashīd. *Fatāwā al-Imām Muḥammad Rashīd Riḍā*. Edited by Ṣalāḥ al-Dīn al-Munjid and Yūsuf Q. Khūrī. Beirut: Dār al-Kitāb al-Jadīd, 2005.

Rowe, William L. "The Problem of Evil and Some Varieties of Atheism." In *The Evidential Argument from Evil*, edited by Daniel Howard-Snyder, 1–11. Bloomington: Indiana University Press, 1996.

Rūmī, Jalāl al-Dīn. *Signs of the Unseen: The Discourses of Jalaluddin Rumi*. Translated by W. M. Thackston, Jr. Boston: Shambhala, 1999.

Ruthven, Malise. *Islam: A Very Short Introduction*. Oxford: Oxford University Press, 1997.

Ruthven, Malise. *Islam in the World*. Oxford: Oxford University Press, 2006.

al-Saffārīnī, Muḥammad b. Aḥmad. *al-Buḥūr al-zākhira fī ʿulum al-ākhira*. Riyadh: Dār al-ʿĀṣima, 2008.

al-Sāmarāʾī, Fāḍil. *ʿAlā ṭarīq al-tafsīr al-bayānī*. Sharjah: Jāmiʿat al-Shāriqa Markaz al-Buḥūth wa-l-Darasāt al-Shāriqa, 2005.

Sardar, Ziauddin. *Reading the Qur'an: The Contemporary Relevance of the Sacred Text of Islam*. Oxford: Oxford University Press, 2011.

Sartre, Jean-Paul. *No Exit and Three Other Plays*. New York: Vintage Books, 1955.

Sartre, Jean-Paul. *Existentialism and Human Emotions*. New York: Philosophical Library, 1957.

Schilling, S. Paul. *God and Human Anguish*. Nashville: Abingdon, 1977.

Schottmann, Sven, and Joseph Camilleri. "Culture, Religion and the Southeast Asian State." In *Culture, Religion and Conflict in Muslim Southeast Asia: Negotiating Tense Pluralisms*, edited by Joseph Camilleri and Sven Schottmann, 1–16. London: Routledge, 2012.

Shāhīn, ʿAbd al-Ṣabūr. *Abī Ādam*. Cairo: Akhbār al-Yawm, 1900.

Shahrour, Muhammad, al-Qasas al-Qur'aani, Qira'at Mu'aasira, Vol. 1, Dar al-Saqi, 2010.

al-Shanqīṭī, Muḥammad Amīn. *Aḍwāʾ al-bayān*. Riyadh: Dār al-Faḍīla; Mansoura: Dār al-Hādī al-Nabawī, 2005.

al-Shaʿrāwī, Muḥammad Mutwallī. *Tafsīr al-Shaʿrāwī*. Cairo: Akhbār al-Yawm, 1991.

Shībah al-Ḥamd, ʿAbd al-Qādīr. *Tahdhīb al-tafsīr wa-tajrid al-taʾwīl*. Riyadh: Muʾassasat ʿUlūm al-Qurʾān, 2011.

Shuqayr, Shafīq b. ʿAbd b. ʿAbd Allāh. *Mawqif al-madrasa al-ʿaqliyya al-ḥadītha min al-ḥadīth al-nabawī al-sharīf*. Beirut: al-Maktab al-Islāmī, 1998.

al-Sijistānī, Abū Dāwūd. *Sunan Abī Dāwūd*. Vol. 2. Edited by Muḥammad ʿAbd al-ʿAzīz al-Khālidī. Beirut: Dār al-Kutub al-ʿIlmiyya, 1996.

al-Sijistānī, Muḥammad b. ʿUzayr. *Kitāb Gharīb al-Qurʾān al-musammā bi-Nuzhat al-qulūb*. Cairo: Maṭbaʿat al-Saʿāda, 1907.

Singer, Richard. *Job's Encounter*. New York: Bookman Associates, 1963.
Sponberg, Alan. "Introduction." In *Maitreya: The Future Buddha*, edited by Alan Sponberg and Helen Hardacre, 1–4. Cambridge: Cambridge University Press, 1988.
Stowasser, Barbara. *Women in the Qur'an, Traditions, and Interpretation*. New York: Oxford University Press, 1994.
Stowasser, Barbara. "Theodicy and the Many Meanings of Adam and Eve." In *Theodicy and Justice in Modern Islamic Thought: The Case of Said Nursi*, edited by Ibrahim M. Abu-Rabi, 1–17. London: Routledge, 2016.
al-Suyūṭī, ʿAbd al-Raḥmān b. al-Kamāl. *al-Durr al-manthūr*. Cairo: Markaz Ḥajar, 2003.
Swinburne, Richard. *Providence and the Problem of Evil*. New York: Oxford University Press, 1998.
al-Ṭabarsī, al-Faḍl b. al-Ḥasan. *Majmaʿ al-bayān*. Beirut: Dār al-Murtaḍā, 2006.
al-Ṭabāṭabāʾī, Muḥammad Ḥusayn. *al-Mīzān*. Beirut: al-Aʿlamī, 1997.
al-Tawayjarī, Ḥammūd b. ʿAbd Allāh. *Itḥāf al-jamāʿa bi-mā jāʾa fī l-fitan wa-l-malāḥim wa-ashrāṭ al-sāʿa*. Vol. 2. 2nd ed. Riyadh: Dār al-Ṣamīʿī, 1993.
al-Thaʿālibī, ʿAbd al-Raḥmān. *al-Juzʾ al-awwal [al-rābiʿ] min Kitāb al-Jawāhir al-ḥisān fī tafsīr al-Qurʾān*. Algiers: A. B. M. al-Turkī, 1905.
al-Ṭībī, ʿUkāsha ʿAbd al-Mannān. *al-Shāyṭān fī ẓilāl al-Qurʾān li-Shaykh Sayyid Quṭb*. Cairo: Maktabat al-Turāth al-Islāmī, 1992.
Tlili, Sarra. *Animals in the Qur'an*. New York: Cambridge University Press, 2012.
Tottoli, Roberto. "Narrative Literature." In *The Wiley Blackwell Companion to the Qur'an*, edited by Andrew Rippin and Jawid Mojaddedi, 562–76. Chichester, UK: Wiley-Blackwell, 2017.
Voltaire. *Candide*. Introduction by Philip Littell. New York: The Modern Library, 1918.
Wadud, Amina. *The Qur'an and Women*. New York: Oxford University Press, 1999.
Wajdī, Muḥammad Farīd. *Muqaddimat ṣafwat al-ʿirfān fī tafsīr al-Qurʾān*. Cairo: Maṭbaʿat al-Shaʿb, 1903.
Weitbrecht, H. U. *The Teaching of the Qur'ān with an Account of Its Growth and a Subject Index*. New York: Macmillan Co, 1919.
Wierenga, Edward. *The Philosophy of Religion*. Chichester, UK: Wiley-Blackwell, 2016.
al-Zamakhsharī, Maḥmūd b. ʿUmar. *al-Kashshāf*. Beirut: Dār al-Maʿrifa, 2009.
Zīnū, Muḥammad. *Rasāʾil al-tawjihāt al-Islāmiyya*. Riyadh: al-Sumiʿī, 1997.

# Index


ʻAbduh, Muḥammad, 6, 19, 21, 85, 116
Abraham, Prophet, 32, 47–48, 80
Abū Zayd, Naṣr Ḥāmid, 53
Adam and Eve, 28, 64, 75, 78, 93, 128; Adam as earthly successor to God, 2, 7–8, 39, 61–62; angels, prostrating before, 5, 13, 19–20, 22, 25, 27–28, 33; Qur'anic text, hadith on Adam invalidating, 16–17; as repentant, 1, 2, 5, 11, 32, 34, 127; Satan, interactions with, 23–27, 33; seduction of, 5, 9–10, 13, 15, 29–31; traditional account of Adamic story, 5–6, 6–14
Al-Aḥbār, Kaʻb, 117
Āl al-Bayt (People of the Prophetic House), 18
*Al-Bidāya wa-l-nihāya* (Ibn Kathīr), 7
Altalib, Hisham, 126
Al-Andalusī, Ibn Ḥazm, 100
angels, 8, 23, 30, 41, 46, 54, 62; angelic belief in the Lord, 56–57; prostration before Adam, 5, 13, 19–20, 22, 25, 27–28, 33; as servants of God, 67–68; souls of the newly dead, questioning, 49, 102–3; special status of Adam, reacting to, 18–19
animals, 43, 57, 58, 110n103, 120; animal offerings to deities, 112; the Devil, entering paradise disguised as an animal, 29; resurrection of, 100, 128; suffering of, Qur'anic explanation for, 71, 90, 94–101
Antichrist, 112, 113. *See also* al-Masīh al-Dajjāl
apocalyptic literature, 3; closure, yearning for, 106, 111, 112–15, 118, 128; problem of evil and, 117–21; textual support as lacking in Qur'an, 115–17
*al-arḍ* (earth), 8
Ashʻarite theology, 18, 66
*asmāʾ* (names), 22–23
*awḥā* (divine communication), 96–97
*awwāb* (devotional return), 82, 89
Al-Balkhī, Abū l-Qāsim, 101

Battle of Ṣiffīn, 53
Bernstein, Richard, 73, 104
Birnbaum, David, 66
Bodman, Whitney S., 24
Brockopp, Jonathan E., 71, 117
*The Brothers Karamazov* (Dostoevsky), 89–90
Buddhism, 113
al-Bukhārī, Muḥammad, 16, 116, 120
*burhān* (evidence), 47

Cabrera, Isabel, 74
Camilleri, Joseph, 44–45
*Candide* (Voltaire), 105
Caplan, Bryan, 46
Cereti, Carlo G., 113
Chomsky, Noam, 22

Al-Dari, Tamim, 121
Dawkins, Richard, 50
Day of Judgment, 55, 78, 80, 96, 118, 125; animals on, 90, 99–100, 101; corrections in behavior before, 103; as Day of Resurrection, 13, 62, 91, 93, 102, 119; divine-satanic communication prior to, 84; God's justice on, 26, 27, 79, 85, 128; paradise and, 10, 90, 99
the Devil, 29, 63, 108n54; Adam and Eve, seduction of, 5, 9, 15, 21; death of Adam, prior knowledge of, 13–14; exile from paradise, 2, 18, 28, 33, 127; prostration before Adam, refusing, 13, 20; as Shayṭān, 23–27, 30, 34, 84–85, 128. *See also* Iblīs
Dews, Peter, 72
*Dialogues concerning Natural Religion* (Hume), 61
Dostoevsky, Fyodor, 89
*al-ḍurr* (sufferings), 86

evil, problem of: divine evil, 3, 71–105; human evil, 3, 61–71; Qur'anic assessment of, 81–89, 117–21
*Evil and the Concept of God* (Madden/Hare), 91

faith, 10, 39, 46, 48, 52, 64, 81, 93; in apocalyptic narratives, 111; evil, testing believer's faith with, 80; God, losing faith in, 83, 89, 102; Job, trying the faith of, 84, 85, 86, 88; *kufr* as disbelief, 51, 52–53; rational *vs.* blind faith, 54, 126; rejection of faith, 55–56; signs for people of faith, 58; spiritual understanding and, 117
Flescher, Andrew Michael, 71
forgiveness, 114, 127; for children of Adam, 32, 34; how to ask for, Adam learning, 6–7; Qur'anic proclamation of, 1, 5, 9, 11
*Fuṣūṣ al-ḥikam* (Ibn ʿArabī), 87

garden, 11, 14; earthly garden, Adam dismissed from, 27–33, 33–34, 127; heavenly garden, mainstream view of, 6–8, 18; Paradise, Garden of, 9, 10, 12, 17, 57, 78
Al-Ghazālī, Abū Ḥāmid, 98
Green, Peter, 65–66

hadith, 115, 119, 121; on animal judgment, 110n103; apocalyptic content of, 117, 120; on Job, 84; Qur'anic text, use of hadith to invalidate, 16–17, 116
Haleem, M. A. S. Abdel, 4, 38n99
Ḥanīfa, Abū, 6
Hare, Peter H., 91
Hashas, Mohammed, 66
Hegel, Georg W. F., 73
Hick, John, 69–70, 94
Holocaust, 72–73, 107n36
Hügel, Friedrich, 72, 73
Hume, David, 61

Iblīs, 84; Adam, refusing to bow before, 13, 22, 23, 25–29, 33; descent to earth, 30; Shayṭān, distinguishing from, 24, 34n1, 128. *See also* Satan
Ibn ʿAbbās, ʿAbd Allāh, 8, 23, 100
Ibn ʿArabī, Abū ʿAbd Allāh Muḥyī al-Dīn, 87, 97
Ibn ʿĀshūr, Muḥammad b. al-Ṭāhir, 17, 19, 23, 29, 85, 100
Ibn Kathīr, Ismāʿīl b. ʿUmar, 6, 7, 8–9, 21, 114
Ibn Qayyim al-Jawziyya, Abū ʿAbd Allāh Muḥammad, 6, 12, 29

Ibn Qutayba, ʿAbd Allāh b. Muslim, 52–53
Ibn Sayyad, Saf, 121
Ibn Taymiyya, Taqī al-Dīn Aḥmad, 17, 45
*ihbiṭū* (divine command to go), 30
Al-Iṣfahānī, Muḥammad ibn Bakr, 12

Jahmite theology, 66
Jesus Christ, 32, 54, 55; al-Mahdi and, 120; as Messiah, 113; second coming of, 112, 114, 115–17, 118
jinn, 26, 95, 106n19; Adam, as predating, 7, 19; creation of, 13, 25; Iblīs as jinn, 24, 25
Job, story of, 32; evil in tale, Qur'anic assessment of, 81–89; family, Job blessed by God with, 108n73; service to God, 63–64, 128
Judas Iscariot, 116

Kellerman, Henry, 48
*khalīfa* (authorized successor), 7–8, 21, 97
Al-Khatib, Mutaz, 66
Kister, Meir J., 24
Kitagawa, Joseph M., 114

Larsson, Goran, 30
Leibniz, Gottfried Wilhelm, 71
Löfstedt, Torsten, 24

Madden, Edward H., 91
Mahdi (eschatological figure), 112, 115, 116, 120–21
Maḥmūd, Muṣṭafā, 72, 115
Maitreya Buddha, 113
al-Masīḥ (Messiah), 120–21
al-Masīh al-Dajjāl (charlatan Messiah), 114, 116, 117, 119, 120–21
Al-Māturīdī, Abū Manṣūr, 6, 30
Al-Māwardī, ʿAlī b. Muḥammad, 21
McAuliffe, Jane, 17
*min ʿindinā,* replacing with *minnā,* 87–88
Moad, Edward Omar, 75
moral evil. *See* human evil under evil
Morrow, John Andrew, 126
Moses, 13, 16, 32, 41, 47, 54
Muhammad, Prophet, 24, 52, 58, 85, 119, 121; Qur'an, on the abandonment of, 125; as redeemer, 115; religion perfected in, 118
Munabbih, Wahb ibn, 117
Muslim ibn al-Hajjāl, 120
Muʿtazilite faith, 18, 66, 83; angels, believing to be capable of sin, 68; animal suffering, on compensation for, 98–99, 100–101; Qur'anic text, rejecting marginalization of, 84

*nafs* (created human soul), 91–92, 93–94, 103, 109n78
natural evil. *See* divine evil under evil
Naʿnāʿ, Ramzī, 15
Nietzsche, Friedrich, 48–49, 72, 73
*No Exit* (Sartre), 129

paradise, 16, 23, 26, 30, 32, 61, 84; Adam as created in, 2, 5, 25; animals, presence of, 100; atonement for sins prior to entering, 65; Day of Judgement and, 10, 90, 99; as dwelling-place of Adam, 2, 17–18, 22; exile of the Devil from, 27–29, 33, 34, 127; story of creation taking place in, 24; in traditional biblical account, 1, 6–14; true happiness found in, 77–78
Pihlström, Sami, 73
predestination, 2, 9, 66, 91, 92
progressivism, negative forms of, 114

Al-Qummī, ʿAlī b. Ibrāhīm, 6
Al-Qurṭubī, Abu ʿAbdullah, 10, 11, 12, 85, 100

Ramahi, Omar M., 126
Al-Rāzī, Fakhr al-Dīn, 7, 22, 29, 68, 84; animals, on final resurrection for,

100–101; Satan, on the capabilities of, 83, 85; satisfaction with God's fate, 88
repentance, 6, 41, 64, 127; Adam as modeling, 2, 32, 34; Adam forgiven and blessed for, 1, 5, 11, 32; evil, repenting for, 65, 79–80
Riḍā, Muḥammad Rashīd, 6, 115, 116, 119, 120
Rowe, William, 94, 99
Rumi, Jalāl al-Dīn, 45, 67, 98, 127

Sabian believers, 118
Al-Ṣādiq, Ja'far ibn Muḥammad, 6
Said Mahran (fictional character), 104–5
Saleh (Qur'anic figure), 55
Sardar, Ziauddin, 53
Sartre, Jean-Paul, 105, 129
Satan, 28, 29, 31, 127; in Adam and Eve story, 9, 10, 15, 16, 27, 30; Iblīs, appearing as, 23, 24, 26, 30; Job, role in tale of, 63–64, 83–89; in Qur'anic story of Solomon, 57, 95. *See also* the Devil; Shayṭān
Schilling, S. Paul, 67, 71
Schottmann, Sven, 44–45
*shafā'a* doctrine of intercession, 115
Shāhīn, 'Abd al-Ṣabūr, 10
Shahrour, Muhammad, 7
Al-Shanqītī, Muḥammad Amīn, 21
Al-Sha'rāwī, Muḥammad Mutwallī, 6, 8, 21, 31, 33, 115–16, 117
*sharr* (harm), 63
Shayṭān, 34, 108n54; descent to earth, 30, 128; Iblīs, distinguishing from, 23–27; Job's suffering, blaming for, 85
Sheba, Queen, 57, 95
Shībah al-Ḥamd, 'Abd al-Qādīr, 9
sin, 8, 10, 24, 65, 68, 115; animals as incapable of, 99, 101; in children, 89–93; freedom of will, as resulting from, 98; holiness *vs.* freedom from sin, 12–13; Job, sin in the story of, 81, 82; original sin, 1, 11, 32, 78; paradise lost due to, 14, 16, 34; repentance of Adam for, 2, 32, 127
Singer, Richard E., 105
Solomon, Prophet, 57, 95
Sponberg, Alan, 113
Stowasser, Barbara, 8, 21
*Sunan Abi Dawud* hadith collection, 121
Al-Suyūṭī, Jalāl al-Dīn, 15, 87
Swinburne, Richard, 65, 72–73, 107n36
Syria, 12, 73

Al-Ṭabarsī, Al-Faḍl b. al-Ḥasan, 95
Al-Ṭabāṭabā'ī, Muḥammad Ḥusayn, 7–8, 18
*tafsīr al-Qur'ān bi-l-Qur'ān* technique, 3
*tafsīr* collections:, 18, 19, 84; of Al-Rāzī, 100; of Ibn 'Abbās, 23; of Ibn 'Āshūr, 17; of Al-Sha'rāwī, 115
*ta'thīm* (sinful talk), 12
Al-Tha'ālibī, Abu Zayd' Abd al-Raḥmān, 19
theodicy, 66, 71, 73, 74, 89, 94, 128
*The Thief and the Dogs* (Maḥfūẓ), 104–5
Tlili, Sarra, 95–96
Ṭuwā, sacred valley of, 13

'Umar, 'Abd Allāh ibn, 7
Umayyads, 53

Voltaire, 105

Wadud, Amina, 8, 34
Wajdī, Muḥammad Farīd, 115
whispers and whispering: newborns, Qur'anic words whispered to, 125; suffering caused by Satan's whispers, 85, 86; tree of life, Satanic whispers regarding, 9, 27; *waswasa* of the Devil, 29–30
Wierenga, Edward, 74

*yasjudu* (devotional submission), 57, 97

# About the Author

**Abla Hasan** is associate professor of practice of Arabic language and culture. She obtained a PhD in philosophy of language in 2013 from the University of Nebraska–Lincoln and an MA in philosophy as a Fulbright grantee from the University of Nebraska–Lincoln in 2009. Dr. Hasan obtained her BA in philosophy from Damascus University, Syria, in 2000, followed by a diploma of high studies from Damascus University in 2001. She is a native speaker of Arabic. She teaches Arabic language and culture at UNL and is the program's coordinator. Her teaching and research focus on Qur'anic studies, Qur'anic hermeneutics, Islamic feminism, and Arabic studies. She has published with *Analize*, *Ar-Raniry*, *JIL*, *Disputatio*, *Al-Manarah*, *E-logos*, and other peer-review international journals. Hasan is the author of: *Decoding the Egalitarianism of the Qur'an: Retrieving Lost Voices on Gender* (Lexington Books, 2019). She is married to Hassan Saleh and is mother to Zein Saleh, Yman Saleh, and Taym Saleh.